ON PRISONS

A GAOLER'S TALES

ON
PRISONS

A GAOLER'S TALES

DANNY McALLISTER

To Sue

'If you stare into the abyss, the abyss stares back at you.'
Nietzsche

Contents

Foreword   xi

How Did I Get Here?   1
Welcome to Prison   5
I Weigh 84kg   13
Open Prisons   16
Resettlement   21
Shit on the Sheets   53
Been on Nights?   57
Nowhere Else to Go   59
Unstill Places   62
Suicide and Self-Harm   73
Sex Offenders   77
Private Prisons Are Wrong   81
Old Places   85
Segs   88
First Command   93
A Bad Day at the Office   101
Back to High Security   109
Going Sick   114
Escape   119

CONTENTS

Dubrava Prison, Kosovo	129
High-Security Prisons	135
Locked into the Legend	141
Do-Gooders	150
Libyan Prisons Post-Revolution	156
Epilogue	169

Foreword

Prisons are fascinating and, at times, appalling places. They reflect society, but are not places in which you would wish to socialise. A well-run prison is only a moment away from chaos. With, as I write, around 82,000 prisoners incarcerated in 130 prisons across England and Wales (almost double the number it was when I joined the Prison Service in 1984), the threat of mayhem is high.

Each prisoner brings his or her criminal history to prison, and that criminality can worsen in prison. Even the best-run prisons can be unsafe. Prison staff strive to achieve a safe establishment: safe to work in, safe to visit and safe to live in. It is a never-ending struggle.

Prisons do not present a cross-section of society but, rather, a distillation of society's most violent, aggressive, vulnerable and mentally unwell individuals.

Be under no illusion – anyone, and I mean anyone, can find themselves breaking the law and ending up in prison. In my time, I have seen doctors, priests, solicitors, barristers, politicians, members of the aristocracy and high-ranking military officers behind bars, as well as the poor and unlucky.

Over the course of my 27-year career as a prison governor, I witnessed the inexorable growth in the number of prisoners and the reduction of resources to deal with this. As an area manager and as the director of high security I managed other prison governors across the country.

Throughout my service, I found myself reflecting on the different aspects of my work. I took to writing down whatever was bothering me, or was of particular interest to me at the time. It could be drugs, riots, escapes or hostage incidents, but it could, also, be the mundane events that happen to people who find themselves in prison. My experiences, and my reflections, are not those of a criminologist, a lawyer, a social worker or a psychiatrist. I was none of those things. I was a gaoler, and these are a gaoler's tales.

How Did I Get Here?

'Whatever you do, don't join the Prison Service.'

So said my father when, as a young man, I first told him of my career plans. My father was a lifelong socialist who had been, at different times in his life, an engineering shop steward in the East End of Glasgow and the Labour mayor of Basingstoke, Hampshire. My father's view was that prisons were offensive places where the poor and the unlucky of society were punished by the rest of society who were not so poor and unlucky. I listened to my father and instead of joining the Prison Service, I went into the Army, which was a respectable career choice and one, as it happens, that would set me up for my future path.

My parents' politics (socialist), religion (Catholic) and social class (working class and Glaswegian to boot) shaped the career choices that I and my brother and sister made. My sister became a social worker and is, in her retirement, still a Labour Party activist. My brother became a printer and stood as the Labour candidate for Basingstoke in the 1983 General Election. When I did join the Prison Service, on leaving the Army, my own politics (left wing), my religion (Catholic) and my class identity (working class, despite the German car, the Labrador and the CBE) shaped the choices I made and the way I governed. The apple doesn't fall far from the tree.

I liked the Army, it played to a young man's idea of life; there was sport, playing at soldiers and going to parties. It's not my style to tell war stories and I'm certainly not one of those 'Army Barmy' people who dine out on military anecdotes and never really leave the officers' mess behind. The Army took me all over the world, to beautiful places like Nepal, Hong Kong and Italy as well as more obvious postings such as Germany, Cyprus and Northern Ireland. As a soldier, I learned to be a leader, honed my resilience and became physically fit, all of which would serve me well in my time as a prison governor. I played sport, gaining a love of rugby that endures to this day, although now as a spectator rather than in the second row.

Then, at the age of 36, by which point I was a major, I found myself approaching the point where I could choose to retire with a pension, albeit a small one. It was time to take stock. I did not want to be Danny McAllister who was born, joined the Army, left the Army and died. So I decided to take the pension and change career. I secured a place to study Social Work at Keele University. Whilst still a serving soldier, and waiting to leave and do the social work qualification, I opened the *Guardian* newspaper one day and saw an advertisement for 'Assistant Governors (Trainee) in the Prison Service'. I looked away, but when I looked again it was still there. I duly applied.

My father had died some four years earlier and so never knew that I had ignored his advice. I hope he would have been reassured that it was, in the end, not such a bad career choice.

The selection process involved a three-day extended interview at the Prison Service Staff College, which was then in Love Lane, Wakefield, just next to the wall of Wakefield prison. I had a month or so left to serve as a soldier and I had already been accepted to do the social work qualification – what could I lose by attending the interview? – so I did.

It had been my intention to do the social work qualification and to work as a probation officer. With hindsight I would have been a terrible probation officer. I lack the type of empathy necessary for the role. When I received the letter saying I had been accepted to train as an AG(T) – the shorthand for Assistant Governor (Trainee) – I decided, with a mental apology to my father, to do so. It turned out to be the best decision I'd made in terms of my professional life.

In September 1984, I reported to the Prison Service Staff College at Wakefield to join the 41st Assistant Governor (T) Course. I began a two-year sandwich course that culminated in the triumph of dropping the (T). The two-year course to train me as an assistant governor started with three months in uniform *pretending* to be a prison officer at Winchester prison and then a posting to a prison, combined with training at the Wakefield College with the rest of the 41st Assistant Governor (T) Course cohort.

My fellow trainees, about 30 of us, were a disparate bunch, with little in common, other than a shared wish to 'do good' and a sense of being fishes out of water. Over the two years we trained together, as well as learning how to calculate a criminal sentence, write a parole report and approve temporary release, we became a group with more in common than we had expected and made the most of our time as reasonably carefree AG(T)s, before the weight of responsibility that came with 'losing the (T)'.

There were the usual shared life experiences enjoyed when you put a group of (reasonably) well-educated men and women together. Fair to say the Henry Boon pub at the end of Love Lane saw as much of the AG(T) course as did the Prison Service Staff College. Somehow, most of us completed the course, due to the professionalism of our tutors more than the application of the students.

My time as a prison governor and, later, as a senior civil servant confirmed what I knew from the Army, that I am a better field officer than a staff officer: Better with people than with paper. However, in all my life working in prisons, with all of the many thousands of people I have met, I can say I've never met a wholly bad person. I have met a lot of people who have done bad things, but no human beings who merit the label 'wholly bad'.

At the end of my training I was set loose on the prison system.

2

Welcome to Prison

Mr A:
The officer made his way along the landing unlocking cell doors.

♪ 'Wey, hey, hey, it's a lovely day – GET UP YOU CUNT – Hey, hey, hey, come out and play – GET UP YOU CUNT – Wey, hey, hey, it's a lovely day – GET UP YOU CUNT – Hey, hey, hey, come out and play – GET UP YOU CUNT – Wey, hey, hey, it's a lovely day – GET UP YOU CUNT – Hey, hey, hey, come out and play – GET UP YOU CUNT – Wey, hey, hey, it's a lovely day – GET UP YOU CUNT – Hey, hey, hey, come out and play – GET UP YOU CUNT!' ♪

It was 1984. I had been in the Prison Service for three months, marginally longer than Mr A, who had been in prison for 11 hours, with another eight years, 364 days and 13 hours to go on his sentence. He had been received in the local prison just after 2000 hours the night before. His trial had lasted 12 days, and he had been found guilty of conspiracy to import drugs and given a nine-year sentence. He was an ex-naval officer who had let greed and the possibility of riches get the better of him. He had been bailed before trial and so last night, the first of his sentence, was his first night in prison. Put in a cell by himself, shellshocked but still functioning, he had awoken to the steady tread, jingle of keys and an offensive couplet from a prison officer. When it was his turn his door was thrown open.

♪ 'Wey, hey, hey, it's a lovely day – GET UP YOU CUNT – Hey, hey, hey, come out and play…' ♪

He jumped up and shouted at the officer, 'Don't call me a cunt.' The officer stopped, keys in hand, and looked at him evenly. 'Who are you?' he said.

'My name is David Carruthers and I came in last night, and I don't like being called a cunt,' the prisoner replied.

The officer regarded him equably and said, 'Right. Well, David Carruthers, you might not be a cunt but the rest of them are.'

♪ 'Wey, hey, hey, it's a lovely day, hey, hey, hey, come out and play – GET UP YOU CUNT.' ♪

He went on his way, unlocking all of the cells on the landing.

Carruthers decided to take a shower, so collected his thin prison towel and, dressed in a tracksuit – prison issue in a fetchingly dull grey – he set off to find the showers. As he passed the officer, he was hailed with a cheery, 'Where the fuck do you think you're going?' He replied, 'I'm off for a shower.' The officer replied, 'It's Tuesday and your shower day is Friday, get back in your cell'. He went back into his cell.

Mr B:
His crimes had been heavy, and he knew he would receive something heavy back, in his sentence. The judge did not disappoint him: he gave him 20 years. Mr B had been on remand in Brixton for many months and knew it was coming, but 20 years was still a shock. He had brought all his belongings from Brixton to court – you never know, you might walk – and he got 20 years. A series of robberies, some armed, what do you expect? Twenty years. He was loaded into a Category A van, he was now officially a 'heavy'

prisoner. He was driven 60 miles to Whitemoor prison, taken out of the van and put in a cell. He had to ask where he was, where he was to spend the next 20 years. Nobody had told him where he was going; he was just put into the Cat A van and despatched.

He was bright enough to know he could do time or he could use time. Within a year he was a model prisoner, the favourite of the education department, on the highest incentive scheme level. If you have to do 20 years, do them as easily as you can. He had been captured, put his hands up, got on with it.

Mr C:
He came in with four Tesco bags full of groceries. It was a Saturday afternoon and he had been out shopping for his family when the police arrested him. He had about £300 in unpaid fines, a court order for his arrest and 14 days in prison in default of payment. He was processed in reception, his wife was phoned to inform her where he was and to ask her to collect the groceries – she never bothered. When he was released, 14 days later, they gave him his shopping back. Some of it was still edible.

Mr D:
It was a Monday evening and the police had brought him straight from court. He was at high risk of self-harming; he was weeping, sobbing uncontrollably. He had been remanded in custody for an assault on his partner. He had some dirty Polaroids in his property – it wasn't clear who the woman was in them, or who the man was. It wasn't clear though the staff studied them carefully and repeatedly. He was frightened and he asked for Prison Rule 43 (segregation from other prisoners), as his solicitor had told him to, so he would be safe. He hoped.

His partner withdrew her complaint. The police accepted the near impossibility of making the assault stick. The Crown Prosecution Service dropped the charges and he was released.

7

Released without the dirty Polaroids, which had mysteriously gone missing. He went back to his partner, for now.

Mr E:

The police wouldn't physically touch him. He was at best lousy and at worst he had AIDS. It was 1988 and everyone was scared of AIDS. The police were wearing full protective suits and face-masks. Their whole bodies were covered except for their eyes. He was in the back of a police van and wouldn't come out. It was fair to say he was under the influence of some substance, and he was less than cooperative towards the police. The police weren't about to go in voluntarily to get him out of the van. The van was parked in the yard of Bristol Prison next to the reception unit. There was a stand-off, and while the paperwork was being done he stayed on the van. Until he was officially a prisoner, the prison staff couldn't deal with him; up until that point he was still a police problem. After about an hour a prison hospital officer came out, dressed normally in a prison officer uniform but with a white jacket. He looked in the back of the police van and said, 'Hello Geordie, back again – come on.' Geordie got out of the van, almost certainly lousy, almost certainly not with AIDS. The police watched him walk into the prison reception with the hospital officer.

Mr F:

He had tried to hang himself in the van that had brought him to prison. It was the eighth recorded time he had tried to hang himself in the 17 years he had been alive. He had tried in his bedroom at home, he had tried in prison on his last sentence as a 16-year-old. Each time he had been found and cut down. The prison did what it could to keep him away from ligatures and ligature points; it was only a matter of time.

Mr G:

He didn't know where he was. He had known, when he went to court that morning, it was possible he could go down for the first time, and he had.

He had shared the same bedroom in the same house on the same Manchester council estate with the same brother for the 15 years since his brother had been born. He had gone to Court from that house, leaving his brother to go to school, two years below him, same school he had attended. He had to go to Court alone; his mum had to work, his dad was no longer around, his mates were nowhere to be seen. His Youth Offending Team worker met him at Court. He went in front of the Court, he had been here before and it held no real terrors, well the routine didn't but the prospect of going down did. He hid it well, very well – he went down with a one-year Detention Training Order – get 12 months do six – he knew the jargon from his mates.

His brother would sleep alone tonight in the bedroom they had always gone to sleep in, always woken up in. They put him in a van and took him, not to Hindley Young Offender Institution where some of his mates were, but to Brinsford Young Offender Institution near Wolverhampton. Hindley Young Offender Institution was too full of his mates, there was no room at the gaol. He didn't know where he was.

Mr H:

The drink had him. Even when he had been in prison for some days and he had physically dried out – the drink had him. He was a neat Scot with polite self-effacing manners when sober. He wasn't even particularly violent when drunk. He was a nuisance when drunk, a thief to get drink. He had been in prison countless times. Everyone knew him in Bedford prison, most liked him. He bounced from gaol to pub to gaol to pub to gaol. He truly tried hard to do well. He truly tried to re-assess, to re-start, start over, draw a line, turn over a new leaf. He was as contrite as a man could be – but the drink had him. Every time he came in, I would go to see him, to say Hello. When first in, always on a short sentence, he was very sorry. As the days passed, and he dried out, he became very hopeful. When he was released, he became very drunk.

Mr J:
He was only doing a few weeks. It would seem like a lifetime. There is a hierarchy in prisons: armed robbers at the top, sex offenders at the bottom, especially paedophiles; and he was below the line of the lowest of the hierarchy, or so the other prisoners decided. On his second day in prison, when he came down for his meal, with the other protected prisoners (none of whom would speak to him due to the nature of his horrific offence), he was assaulted by a servery worker, who hit him on the head with a ladle. The 'boing' reverberated around the gaol and there were dozens of people there, but– 'nobody' saw the assault. The nature of his offence was such that every prisoner could look down on him. He had deliberately killed his girlfriend's puppy with a hammer, after she left him.

Mr K:
He was remanded on two counts of murder, and the victims had been known to him. He was kept in the prison hospital as he was at risk of self-harm and was vulnerable. He was a serving soldier and I spoke with him most days. He knew the reality of his future. He never got to trial, and he left a note. He told me he couldn't face a future without feeling the sun on his back, without going for a run in a wood, without a glass of wine and the arms of someone who loved him, and he left a note saying so. I had tried to tell him that everything passes, nothing was forever, it would get better – but he was insightful and knew, and he left a note.

Mr L:

He was a big bloke. He was an aggressive big bloke. He had an anger in him that shone out, or in; mostly in, but there was a sufficient amount left to shine out to frighten people. He was remanded for killing a schoolboy, with sexual overtones. Nobody liked him, and *he* especially didn't like him. He appeared before me, the wing governor, on some application or other. Staff were aware that he might attack the wing governor so they made sure that there were enough of them present. He was angry, as usual, he was big, as usual, he was threatening, as usual – he made to move aggressively towards me. Staff moved quickly, gladly and professionally to restrain him and remove him to the segregation unit. Everybody, everybody including him, breathed a sigh of relief that he was going to the segregation unit. There, he might get some peace from the taunting of some prisoners, the coldness of some staff, but, mostly, some peace from himself. In his heart he knew it didn't work like that.

Mr M:

He was halfway through the procedures to change his gender. Hormones had given him breasts but he had not yet had any surgery. The prison wasn't sure what to do with him, but the paperwork said he was a man, so he was in a male prison. He was before me, as the adjudicating governor, on a charge of snogging another prisoner, on the prison's main corridor, in front of everyone. His defence was that it was natural. My response was, 'So is urinating, but I wouldn't want you doing that on the main corridor in front of everyone either!' I admonished him. He accepted this with good grace.

Mr N:

He had a roll-on deodorant bottle up his bum. Reception staff challenged him as to his ataxic gait (he was walking with his feet

18 inches apart, like a recently dismounted cowboy). He produced the deodorant bottle when he knew the game was up. When staff unscrewed the top, gingerly, it was full of pills and some cannabis resin. He had taken a chance; it hadn't worked. He knew he'd be able to get drugs on the wing, but it was still a blow to lose his stash.

3

I Weigh 84kg

'I weigh 84kg,' he said, as I was handcuffed to him.

Then he said it again, and every minute thereafter, as we travelled from Wormwood Scrubs prison to Winchester Prison – a two-hour journey. The reason for the transfer was overcrowding at Scrubs, and empty cells at Winchester. Quite simply, prisoners were taken to wherever there were spaces; forget about proximity to their home, family or support networks.

It was an odoriferous journey from Scrubs to Winchester, as he clearly had difficulty with his personal hygiene.

I felt sorry for myself, not him, which probably tells you more about me than him, but I was young and selfish: I'm older now.

I was, pretty much, at the bottom of the food chain; an assistant governor trainee, pretending to be a prison officer for three months, as the first part of my training.

I had been handcuffed to this man, because somebody had to be. Generally, prisoners are handcuffed to each other, in pairs, but if there is an odd number, the most junior prison officer, me in this case, would be handcuffed to a prisoner for transfer. The other prisoners had made it clear that they did not wish to be handcuffed to this man, the prison officers did not wish to be handcuffed to this man, and so, therefore, it fell to me.

He was a young man, perhaps mid-twenties and heavily built. As he completed his prison sentence at Winchester, a short sentence but one of a series of such sentences that he served, I saw him around the prison. He was given a wide berth by other prisoners, due to his inability to take care of himself and the fact that he would repeat his weight like a mantra.

I don't know what became of him. He just got lost in the mix. He was an unremarkable example of the people in prison with mental health difficulties.

According to figures released in 2017, 15% of men and 25% of women in prison have symptoms indicative of psychosis, compared to 4% of the general population. 23% of men and 49% of women in prison are identified as suffering from both anxiety and depression, compared to 15% of the general population. The spectrum of mental illness manifested in prisons ranges from the mildly inconvenient to the hugely disabling. The degree of probability of danger, both to self and others, goes from highly unlikely to almost certain.

We cannot begin to treat dangerous and severely personality-disordered people in prison, with our present level of professional training. We treat most of the other treatable, if not curable, mental illnesses that people held in prison suffer with.

How mental illness manifests itself varies enormously. According to the 2017 figures, 21% of men and 46% of women in prison have attempted suicide at some point, compared to 6% of the general population. Lest we put this down solely to the conditions in prison, another illuminating statistic is that men who are recently released from prison are eight times more likely to kill themselves than the general population, and women recently released from prison are 36 times more likely to kill themselves. The statistics do not begin to tell the story. The reality for those lost in the system, and suffering from debilitating mental illness, is too horrible to contemplate; yet not only is it witnessed every day in prison, it is also on the increase. As the prison population increases, so too does the number of people with mental illness held in prison.

For prison staff, this means having to deal with situations for which they are not trained. One morning, in Whitemoor prison, officers opened a cell to find the walls covered in globules of human fat, with the blood streaking the cell walls, where the man had gouged the fat out of his body, and thrown it around the cell. How staff can be trained to deal with this type of incident, or even have the skills or knowledge to address this level of distress, is beyond me. You learn on the job to compartmentalise these experiences – to put them into a corner of your mind, as you would in the Army, and move on. There is a job to be done.

While there is a much higher suicide rate among prisoners than in the general population, a much larger number of individuals are saved from death inside prison by the courageous intervention of staff. This goes unacknowledged.

It is not only staff who have to deal with people with acute mental illness in prison, so too do fellow prisoners. Their response can vary, from the predatory, through derision, past impatience, to a rare kind of caring, if lucky.

In the foreword to a Prison Reform Trust paper of 2005, Erwin James, himself a former prisoner, stated, 'On the wing there was plenty of evidence of behaviour brought on by mental distress.'

I was grateful, then, as a young assistant governor trainee, to have part of my training in the form of a placement in a mental hospital, before many mental hospitals (or asylums) were closed down. Consequently, there are few asylums for those who struggle to thrive or cope in the community, and what I do know is that prison is the worst place for these individuals.

I do not doubt that there are, right now, in many prisons across the country, people, just as the man who weighed 84kg, who should not be in the prison system.

Shame on us.

4

Open Prisons

As I neared the end of the first 10-week part of the Assistant Governor Trainee Course at the Prison Service Staff College, Love Lane, Wakefield, I awaited my fate. I had expressed no preference as to where I should be posted so had no idea of the likely outcome. Now, sitting opposite me was the man who would decide my first posting as an assistant governor in the Prison Service. I watched him consult the course tutors before pronouncing his decision. 'Leyhill Prison.' I'd never heard of it.

I nodded. 'Thanks,' I said. Little did I know that I had just been given a golden ticket and a job that most governor grades would have killed for. As one old stager governor said to me, 'They should take leave off you for working there'.

Open prison might sound like a contradiction in terms. What about the adage that 'happiness is door shaped'? Not a bit of it. I soon came to realise that this cynical attitude to prison offered, at best, a very temporary solution to some very complex issues. You can lock the problem away, but it doesn't go away, it's still there when you unlock the door. It is not in the individual's interest, nor society's interest, to adopt a 'because I say so' approach.

Instead, I came to realise, during more than three years at

Leyhill, exactly how effective and beneficial these types of prison can be. They are particularly effective at preparing long-term prisoners for re-entry into the community and as a cost-effective way to curtail liberty, where each man is his own gaoler. The poet Richard Lovelace was right; it is not walls or bars that make a prison, but the realisation that each person has to face up to the reality of their actions and needs to do better, or take the consequences.

I rolled up to Leyhill Prison in Gloucestershire, set amid many acres of rolling countryside and mature trees. A gentler approach to imprisonment would have been hard to find. The prison housed 300 prisoners in the huts put up as an American Second World War hospital. Of the 300 men, almost a third were serving a life sentence. These lifers were, they hoped, nearing release from the custodial part of their life sentences. Leyhill would provide them with a final assessment of risk. A final hurdle to surmount.

The governor was a thoughtful and caring man who was nobody's fool, but understood the importance of giving responsibility to those in his charge. One day, he told me, 'There is nothing to stop all the prisoners in this prison from forming into three ranks and marching out the gate with pipes and drums playing'. He said this as we were in his office, looking out at the gardens where prisoners were gardening, or strolling individually and in groups. The gardens, including a huge market garden complex, employed most of Leyhill's prisoners.

The fact that so very few prisoners absconded is testimony to the enlightened self-interest that meant that the prisoners realised their good fortune, felt respected and behaved accordingly. The philosophy behind open prisons was the antithesis of the 'bang them up and give them nothing and, if they complain, take it away from them' attitude that can be tempting to apply when faced with difficult human beings. Each type of prison requires different skills and attitudes from its staff; there is no 'one size fits all' approach to working in the Prison Service. However, the ability to listen to those in our charge, and the need for some compassion, which I learned from my early governors, were attributes that served me well in all of the prisons I worked in subsequently; from the high-security estate to the open estate. It was harder to operate in a prison where you could not just put people away behind their door. You left them out in the open prison to face their problems; they had to face up to them, but so did I.

I owe much to the two Leyhill governors I served under. They treated me with kindness and forbearance.

At one time we had a prisoner who was highly educated but who could not accept the fact that he was in prison as a punishment for the wrongs he had done to others, nor did he accept that he was not entitled to privileged treatment. I would have given him the shortest of shrift, but the governing governor talked him through the reality of his situation with the patience of a saint – and the prisoner finally got it. My way would have made him bitter; the governor's way made him better. The prisoner had to take responsibility for the actions that had brought him to prison without the kind of learned helplessness that some parts of the prison system can engender. This man had been a successful businessman who, when times got tough, had been liberal with his approach to book-keeping and tax liability so, in his eyes, he was not really a criminal. He became aware, under the governor's gentle direction, that a criminal is whoever the courts decide is a criminal.

Given that open prisons run on trust, there were few who failed to take responsibility for their actions.

The experienced principal officer who guided me through my early years in the job reminded me of the subaltern/platoon sergeant relationship in the Army, where the (theoretically) senior grade learns a great deal from the junior grade. I was approached, as I walked around the prison, by a prisoner who sought my guidance as to whether he was entitled to home leave, and I gave an off the cuff answer. I was at my desk, later the same day, when the principal officer came back from lunch and he said to me, 'Did you tell a prisoner that he was entitled to home leave?'

'Yes, shouldn't I have?'

'No. You got that wrong, and now there are another hundred prisoners outside, waiting to apply for the home leave to which you said they were entitled.'

I thought he was joking. However, when I went to open the door, I found a very long queue of prisoners, all waiting to apply for the home leave to which I had, wrongly, said they were entitled. You can imagine how popular I was when I explained to them that I had given out duff info. That principal officer was known to the prisoners as 'The Mirror Man', since, whenever he was asked something 'on the hoof' by a prisoner, he always replied, 'I will look into it.'

Now I understood why.

Open prisons don't work for everyone. I recall one man who had committed an extremely brutal murder when drunk and, after many years in the prison system, had finally made it to open prison as a prelude to final testing and release. He was returned to closed prison when he was found in the Leyhill visits room drinking whisky that was concealed in the drink smuggled in by his mother. After 20 years in prison, he had still not learned his lesson, nor, it appeared, any lessons at all.

On another occasion, a man with a history of dysfunctional sexual attitudes to women (he had committed the murder of a woman) was called to my office. I was to inform him of a parole decision that would lengthen his time in prison by years, but I was incapable of holding his attention whilst a woman walked past the window and his attention switched to her, only returning his eyes to me when she had moved out of sight.

Another life-sentenced prisoner, many, many years into his life sentence, told me that he never wanted to be let out because he would only be back via the nearest pub. He had a gift for painting perfect copies of great paintings and he was happy where he was. He died in prison.

I learned my so-called gaol craft in Leyhill open prison, preparing me for what was to come later in my career. Mostly, I remember Leyhill prison as a place of lightness and hope, though I suppose a prisoner's view might be different.

5

Resettlement

The Prison Service in England and Wales has a statement of purpose to guide those who work in it:

> We keep in custody those committed by the courts. Our duty is to look after them with humanity and to help them lead law-abiding and useful lives in custody and after release.

Security is essential for the efficient running of any prison system, but it is not enough. For an ex-prisoner to be returned to society, reformed and able to contribute and engage, it is essential that resettlement work is done to reduce his risk of reoffending and improve his life chances. How do we ensure this eventuality?

In 1988, whilst a junior governor grade at Leyhill, I worked with an experienced principal officer in the lifer unit. In fact, the two of us *were* the lifer unit, responsible for the final testing of 120 life-sentenced prisoners and their preparedness for release into the community. It was a 'prima donna' job, with status within the prison and a raised profile for those occupying the posts. One day, we were surprised to hear that we had received an award from the Butler Trust. The Butler Trust, a charity that identifies 'ordinary work extraordinarily well done' in prisons, had awarded us their top annual prize of an overseas scholarship.

The scholarship allowed me and my colleague to travel and to learn from other prison systems. We decided to visit prisons in Europe, specifically in Sweden, The Netherlands, Germany and Hungary, to see the work going on in those countries to prepare prisoners for release. We were keen to learn from other prison systems and to bring back good practice that we could use in our ongoing work at Leyhill.

I believed then, as I do now, that for most prisoners, how they are prepared for release is crucial to determining their chance of becoming a contributing citizen and staying away from crime when they are released from prison. Often, the commencement of a prison sentence is marked by the delivery of an angry and incompetent individual into a prison. Too often, the completion of a prison sentence is marked by the delivery of an angry and incompetent individual out of prison and back into society. This is a tragedy.

The process of incarceration can be divided into the two pillars of Security and Control, while the release process can be seen in terms of Preparation and Testing. Efficient incarceration is not newsworthy; it is a service to the public that, in the majority of prisons in England and Wales, is delivered with skill, technical excellence and humanity. This is what allows the service to move on to apply a release process in tandem with the incarceration process. Incarceration is necessary but it is not enough.

There are three elements that contribute to the harm that prison does. These elements, which work against successful release, are feelings of:

powerlessness,
hopelessness and
uselessness.

If this triad of misery can be countered or removed, then, and only then, can imprisonment be a positive process.

Powerlessness: Too often when a person enters a period of imprisonment he enters a period when he has no power over his life: he is a slave to the system. Successful rehabilitation should operate to allow the imprisoned person to retain, or gain, some power over the direction in which his life will proceed.

Hopelessness: Too often a person commencing a period of imprisonment experiences a sense of hopelessness and there does not seem to be a foreseeable end to the misery. Successful rehabilitation should aim to structure the imprisonment career in such a way that hopelessness is replaced with a planned, structured programme.

Uselessness: Many people entering prison do not have the necessary skills to enable them to earn an honest living post release. The period of imprisonment can be used to provide these skills, so that upon release the person can, should he choose, earn a living without recourse to crime.

We knew, from our work with the lifers in Leyhill, that the trick was to combine efficient incarceration with efficient preparation for eventual release, so that, when he returns to society, a prisoner is able to contribute.

Our visits to prisons in Europe would allow us to see where good practice existed and could be imported into our own work. These were some of the prisons we visited and what we learned.

OSTERAKER CLOSED NATIONAL PRISON, SWEDEN

Osteraker Prison is 35km north of Stockholm and probably best known for hosting a live concert in 1972 by Johnny Cash and his band; a recording of the concert was released on an album the following year. We knew that Osteraker was doing groundbreaking work with prisoners, including drug misusers and addicts, and we wanted to see how this work might provide useful learning for us at home.

During the mid-1970s the Swedish National Prison and Probation Administration had recognised the fact that drug misuse was a major problem within prisons. Approximately 30% of sentenced prisoners in Swedish prisons, at that time, were drug misusers. The administration decided to do something positive about this problem for the benefit of prisoners and for society in general, and so specialist drugs units were set up in several prisons.

We had read that the treatment programme at Osteraker Prison was the most comprehensive, and so agreed we should see it for ourselves. When we visited, at the start of our European tour, the prison housed 160 prisoners. Apart from those on normal location there were 60 prisoners housed in the drug unit. The unit was divided into six self-contained sections, each with 10 prisoners, staffed during the working day by an assistant governor, one senior officer and three officers, with one principal officer for all six sections. With such high staffing levels, far in excess of anything in the UK, it was clear that the Swedish system could achieve superior results in terms of treatment and rehabilitation.

As we sat drinking coffee in the director's office, he told us, 'We do not have slums in Sweden, but it is possible for a person to live in a drug-induced *mental* slum.' The director told us that a prisoner could not be forced to take part in the treatment programme, he had to apply, and could be transferred to Osteraker from other prisons to take part in the programme. Any prisoner had to have at least eight months of his sentence left to serve, to make the treatment likely to succeed.

Key to the treatment model was the daily urine test. The way in which a sample was obtained was simple, straightforward and foolproof. An initial test would be carried out on the sample at the prison and any positive samples sent away for more accurate testing. This was seven years before the introduction of urine testing in UK prisons, and a decade before the opening of specialist drug treatment units in some of them.

We then toured the prison. The prisoners' rooms were much the same size as in the UK, containing a bed, table, chair, shelving and storage space. TVs were permitted, and could be bought or rented from the prison (it would be almost ten years before in-cell television was available as an 'earnable privilege' to prisoners in the UK). Prisoners could wear their own clothing, another privilege that would not be extended to those in UK prisons until some years later. Education was prioritised, as were workshop activities – mainly carpentry and textile work. The workshops were not designed on a production line basis; rather, the prisoner would be rewarded for making an article from start to finish, which built his self-confidence. Group meetings on the unit could involve role play, discussions, problem solving, learning social skills, individual progress and constructive criticisms of each other. A psychologist participated in most of these sessions, along with all grades of staff working in the section.

Along with most modern prison services, the Swedish service recognised that keeping in contact with his family was crucial to a prisoner's successful resettlement. In the drug unit visits could take place each weekend, on Saturday and Sunday from 0900–1530 hours. Conjugal visits were allowed with wives or girlfriends and the visits took place on the living units, in the prisoner's room. For those prisoners whose wives had a long distance to travel, a flat could be provided within the prison. The prisoner and his wife could stay in the flat overnight. This remains unheard of in UK prisons.

Apart from letters and phone calls, prisoners were allowed a one-day home leave, escorted by one of the section staff, after they had served a quarter of their sentence – or two months, whichever was the greater. Two months later a similar home leave could take place. On this second home leave the prisoner would be allowed out for 48 hours. Two months after that he would be allowed out for 72 hours home leave and this was then repeated every two months. One week prior to going on home leave, the prisoner could, possibly, be given anti-drug or alcohol medication.

Another interesting condition of release was that prisoners had to have saved 837 kroner before being allowed to take home leave. The cost of living is high in Sweden. If the prisoner had no home to go to, the prison would pay for the accommodation but the prisoner would always be expected to pay for his food and his travel. This level of home leave provision contrasted markedly with that in the UK, although, at Leyhill and as part of final testing before release, the granting of home leave was more generous than in other, closed, prisons. At Osteraker, on return, a prisoner could expect to be urine tested and breathalysed. If a prisoner gave positive samples he would be removed from the unit and sent to another prison. In some cases, if circumstances were considered favourable, the prisoner might be allowed to return to the drug unit after two months had elapsed. Because each failure was seen to reflect on the unit, each prisoner going on home leave was under pressure from his peers not to abuse the privilege.

At that time, prisoners in Sweden were released automatically after serving two thirds of their sentence. On application, and if reports were favourable, it was possible to be released after serving half of the sentence. We learned that this also applied to prisoners in the drug unit, but additionally, if it was thought to be beneficial, prisoners in the drug unit could be transferred out of prison to live in a drug support unit in the community. The prisoner, when in this unit, would still be deemed to be serving his sentence.

Overall, we were impressed by the positive atmosphere at Osteraker, with staff and prisoners working together, despite some abuse of the programme; for example, the occurrence of trafficking in urine (something we would experience in UK prisons, when mandatory drug testing was introduced there in 1996). Prisoners who knew they were 'clean' would sell their urine to be passed off as the urine of someone who had been using drugs, so that their result would be a negative one. Staff were aware of this trafficking and countered it by vigilance. The active and searching attitude to drug abuse adopted by the Swedish prison system, which was in evidence at Osteraker, was in stark contrast to the ineffective hand-wringing approach in UK prisons at that time. It would be some years before the UK Prison Service caught up and introduced proper policies and initiatives to address the increasing challenge of drug abuse within our prisons.

HUDDINGE CLOSED LOCAL PRISON, SWEDEN

Huddinge prison is situated some 12km south of Stockholm. It was built in 1983, one of 30 new local prisons built as part of a Swedish government initiative to localise many prison establishments, so that prisoners could remain in their home area. This was aimed at supporting prisoners to build and retain meaningful contact with those external agencies which could aid their resettlement. It contrasted and, we felt, compared favourably with what we were seeing in UK prisons at that time. In the UK, new-build prisons were, typically, being built in remote areas, away from the towns to which prisoners would be returning, and were larger than the old local gaols in order to achieve economies of scale. At the time of our visit, Huddinge was one of six local prisons in the vicinity of Stockholm and housed 42 prisoners, aged from 17 upwards. Although the population was small, the throughput was quite high, with between 200 and 250 prisoners passing through the prison gates each year. Most prisoners at Huddinge were serving a sentence of one year or less, although prisoners serving longer could apply for transfer there as they prepared for release. It was made clear to us, when we visited Huddinge, that the purpose and main theme of the prison was preparation for release. The philosophy of Huddinge was explained to us by the director, and was that, 'Correctional treatment in an institution shall be so designed as to promote the adjustment of the inmate to society and to counteract the detrimental effect of deprivation of liberty. Treatment should be directed from the outset towards measures which prepare the inmate for existence outside the institution. Preparation should begin in good time before release.'

He went on to explain that, for the majority of prisoners, active preparation for release started upon conviction. Indeed, treatment plans would often have been formulated prior to conviction while the prisoner was awaiting trial in the remand prison.

The prisoners we met at Huddinge had not been sent there by chance, but because of their individual resettlement needs. The day-to-day programme at Huddinge was specifically geared to dealing with prisoners who needed help with their basic education, especially in the areas of English, Swedish and mathematics. No such bespoke provision existed then, nor does it exist now, in the UK and we were impressed by what we heard and saw. The staffing at Huddinge was generous; for 42 prisoners there were 37 staff, of whom 17 were officers. This made Huddinge an expensive prison; it had been expensive to build and it was expensive to run. Everything we saw at Huddinge demonstrated a genuine commitment to resettlement, and it was clear that only the provision of finance allowed the impressive philosophy to be carried out in practice.

We were given a copy of the Huddinge Handbook, which told us that, 'The work governs the architecture – it is built on the lines of a normal home and working environment in society.' The place did, indeed, feel more 'normalised' than anything we had seen at home. The living accommodation was divided into five units of eight prisoners, plus one unit of two prisoners. Each cell was of a similar size, slightly larger than those found in the UK, and there was an additional smaller, separate room large enough to house the toilet and hand basin. Each prisoner was allowed his own TV and there was piped radio in each cell. Each unit of eight cells had its own kitchen, where prisoners prepared their own breakfast every day. There was one shower for the use of each unit of eight prisoners. Every cell had electrical sockets and when I asked about the potential for abuse of these, I was told by a straight-faced director that only once had there been any: when a prisoner tried to make love to the socket! He did add, also with a straight face, that the prisoner had done it 'only once'. There were no bars on any of the windows at Huddinge – indeed no bars anywhere in the entire prison. All windows were double glazed, the inner pane being toughened glass. The decor and furnishings throughout the unit were tasteful and well looked after by the prisoners. For example, cell window curtaining – supplied by the prison – was of excellent quality with a wide range of patterns available. To add to the 'normality' of the environment, prison staff didn't wear uniform, making it difficult for us to tell staff, prisoners and visitors apart. There was also a gymnasium, a well-equipped weights room and two saunas. The Swedish authorities viewed the provision of a sauna for prisoners as perfectly acceptable; later in my career, when the Prison Service bought prefabricated accommodation units from Scandinavia, we would arrange for the saunas to be removed before the units were brought into use. They simply would never have passed the public acceptability test in our society.

At Huddinge, prisoners were unlocked at 0630 and remained unlocked until 2000 hours. Within that time period they were expected to study and work for a full eight hours. Educational classes and time in the workshops were rotated between the groups of prisoners. The education department was extremely well equipped, and on top of classroom studies, social and life skills were taught in a modern kitchen. When we visited, the kitchen was being well used by prisoners supervised by staff.

There were two main workshops at Huddinge, both carpentry, each equipped with up-to-date industrial machinery. The workshops were not run on a production line basis, there was no production timescale and no question of profit-making as the lead motive. Each prisoner could make a complete item from start to finish, from picture frames to drop leaf dining tables. The items that we saw produced were of very good quality. Apart from teaching the prisoner new skills, the reasoning behind this type of work was the same as in Osteraker; that is, to show the prisoner that he could produce something useful and of good quality, so boost his self-confidence and self-esteem. The quality of the regime facilities was superior to what we were used to in UK prisons, but the greatest difference was in the expectation that prisoners would spend a full day in activities, replicating a working day out in the community, which they achieved. In too many of our prisons, then and now, restrictive staff working practices and a lack of 'regime grip' shrink the working day for prisoners to little more than an hour or so either side of a very long lock up over lunchtime. This reduces significantly the time available for any meaningful resettlement work.

Finding employment in readiness for release was an important part of the resettlement process at Huddinge. Whenever possible, employment was found some months before the actual discharge, and in these cases, if the prisoner was considered suitable, he would be allowed to work outside the prison. He would then receive the going rate for the job from the firm and his money would be dealt with as if he were not in prison i.e., he would pay taxes, he would pay for his family and so forth. He would also then have to pay for his keep in prison, albeit at a much-reduced rate from what he would have to pay to look after himself outside prison. He would also be expected to start paying off outstanding debts, fines and so forth, with staff advising him on how best to handle his money. When we visited, there were 10 prisoners of the 42 at Huddinge working out of the prison. Whilst UK prisoners in open prisons could, and can, work in the community, the concept of this being extended to prisoners in local prisons, as a prelude to release, was new to us and showed real commitment to getting resettlement right. The financial dimension to these arrangements remains in the 'too difficult' box for us; over the years politician have suggested that prisoners should pay for their own keep, and that of their dependants, but our complex tax and benefits rules make such arrangements disproportionately expensive to administer.

We also heard how spending time outside the prison confines was considered very important from the time a prisoner arrived at Huddinge. An officer could be permitted to take up to three prisoners on various outside activities, for example fishing, canoeing or walking in the surrounding woodlands. Shopping and visiting sporting events were particularly popular. These activities took place outside the prisoner's working day, normally in the evenings and at weekends, and could last up to six hours at a time, subject to staff availability. In the UK, such activities were restricted to young offenders' institutions and, even then, were already being viewed as wasteful and unpalatable to the general public. These days, the shrinking of available resources has led to almost all 'flexible' work in our prisons falling by the wayside.

At Huddinge, prisoners were not allowed to forget their family responsibilities and close contact with their families was maintained from the very beginning of their sentence. Prisoners could have a two-hour visit every week outside the working day i.e. in the evenings and at weekends (again, in contrast to our own system where visits eat into the working day, taking prisoners away from work, education and the like). Visits took place in private rooms, unsupervised, and therefore conjugal visits were seen as the norm. Home leave provision was similar to that at Osteraker, demonstrating the emphasis on looking outwards and forward, not inwards and backward. In addition to this, outside employment agencies and accommodation agencies visited the prison every fortnight, giving their assistance wherever possible.

As in all Swedish prisons, however, one of the main concerns at Huddinge was drug and alcohol misuse and how to address it. The methods used here were those employed at Osteraker, i.e., urine tests and breathalysers, and the consequences of repeatedly failing the tests were equally harsh. If a prisoner was proved to have taken drugs or abused alcohol on more than two occasions, the governor could, and did, transfer him to a national prison, where he would live under a much harsher regime.

What we saw at Huddinge was impressive. The accommodation and facilities were excellent and the commitment of all staff to the resettlement process was clear. Equally clear to us, though, was that Huddinge was no easy option for its prisoners. They were not allowed to hide away from reality, they had to work hard at their studies, they had to work hard at their release plan and they had to work at the problem of their drug or alcohol abuse. For a prisoner who had been in prison many times before, this prison was a test of character. At Huddinge, they had failures, failure with drug abusers, failure with home leaves, failure with escapes. The important point was that the staff were not demoralised; rather they looked to their successes, of which there were many.

It was unfortunate that, when we visited, reconviction statistics were not available to us and so we could not assess the success of Huddinge against the most important measure: did it stop people reoffending? What was clear, however, was that the resources provided for prisoners, the positive attitude of the staff and the whole ambience of this closed prison compared more than favourably with the best of our open prisons and there was much that we could learn from this optimistic and forward-looking approach.

From Sweden we travelled to Germany, at that time West Germany, where our next visit was to:

BRUCHSAL PRISON, GERMANY

Bruchsal prison is some 65km south of Stuttgart. Built in 1848 in the 'Pennsylvania' style, at the time of our visit it housed 400 long-term adult prisoners with a further 70 in a *freigangerheim* outside the main prison wall (a *freiganger* is a prisoner who is allowed out of the prison during the day and returns at night). In total contrast to Leyhill, with its absence of physical security and relaxed ethos, Bruchsal had security features that included dogs, cameras and a walkway on the top of the prison wall patrolled by officers armed with submachine guns. The staff also had radios, binoculars, searchlights and telephones, housed in turrets placed at strategic points around the top of the wall. For easy identification, the numbers of the cells, and the rows, were painted on the outside of each building.

One interesting consequence of the high level of security at Bruchsal and many other German prisons was a real fear of hostage-taking incidents. We learned that, during the last two years in that region of Germany there had been six major hostage incidents, but that such incidents seemed, at the time of our visit, to be on the decline. We were told that no hostage takers' demands had been met, nor was it envisaged that they ever would be. In UK prisons, and described in a later chapter, we saw the same phenomenon; as we made escape more difficult, the frequency of other incidents, including hostage taking, increased, as if the need to protest and push against the system didn't go away, it just found other outlets.

Facilities at Bruchsal were excellent; they included a gymnasium, a large grass area for recreation, a football ground, a hospital, workshop complexes, education complexes and a large market garden area outside the prison wall. All prisoners had single cells, with the door from each cell opening outwards to remove the potential for prisoners to barricade their cells or hold hostages. We were familiar with these anti-barricade doors, which were also used in prisons at home, and had transformed, with a simple design tweak, the ability to enter a cell when a prisoner is on the other side of the door trying to prevent it.

There were no individual TV sets allowed in Bruchsal. Food was good, with staff and prisoners eating the same food from the same kitchen, thus reducing the number of frivolous complaints about food. In UK prisons, this would, even in 2017, be an unacceptable practice for most prison staff. For some reason, our prison staff have an aversion to eating the same food as prisoners and this nut has proved exceptionally difficult to crack.

All but the most dangerous of prisoners were allowed to keep in touch with their families and friends by telephone on a regular basis. The prisoner had to pay for the calls out of his earnings. Prisoners were entitled to a minimum of one visit per month of between three and four hours duration. Visits were taken in what seemed to be private rooms; that is, the rooms were private in that no other prisoner could observe. However, one complete wall of the visits room was a two-way mirror that allowed staff, sitting at tables, to observe all visits all the time. This gave prisoners a feeling of privacy, although all were aware of the two-way mirror and the observation by staff. We didn't recommend that this system be adopted in our own prisons; it seemed more difficult for staff to supervise visits properly and to intervene when necessary. All visitors to prisoners were given a rub-down search (as in the UK, female visitors were searched by a female officer) and all visitors had to pass through a metal detector before the visit took place. Prisoners also passed through a metal detector on the way into the visit and on the way out of the visit.

The education programme was extensive, ranging from the basics to degree level, and social workers attended the prison regularly, to lead therapeutic group discussions. This was something we hadn't seen before, but we had no real sense of the purpose, nor of any evaluation of the benefits to prisoners nor to the wider prison.

A very positive area of the prison was the workshop complex, where the emphasis was on training and not production. Prisoners were able to take a three-year apprenticeship in one of the trades on offer. The trades taught were printing, bookbinding, plumbing, locksmithing (surprisingly), carpentry, construction and civil engineering, and computer programming. For all of these trades, the successful prisoner received a certificate at the end of the first, second and third (final) years. There was no indication on the certificate as to where it had been earned so that a prisoner could carry on with his training on release should his sentence be too short to complete the course. Similarly, if a prisoner was sent to prison having obtained the first or second year training certificates in a trade, he would be able to complete his training in prison. This enlightened thinking was impressive and in advance of our approach in the UK. Within five years, though, education and training in UK prisons would be outsourced to colleges and other specialist providers, with the opportunity to align delivery with what was available to students in the outside community.

We learned that prisoners in Germany completed their sentence within one prison complex, with contact with the outside being given back to the prisoner in a gradual and planned manner. When the time was right, a prisoner would be able to work on the market gardens, outside the prison wall, supervised by an officer. This was seen as an important part of the release process, necessary before staff could decide whether or not a prisoner could work outside the prison unsupervised. If he could, he would be transferred to the freigangerheim, or hostel, outside the prison wall. Whilst on the freigangerheim a prisoner would be required to work to pay for his food and accommodation, but also to support his wife and family, so the responsibility for himself and for his family was given back to him as a wage earner. At Bruchsal, the freigangerheim housed 70 prisoners, two to a room. The amenities were basic, though adequate: cooking facilities, TV room, association room and laundry room. Opportunities for family contact were quite generous while the prisoner was on the freigangerheim. Initially, a freiganger prisoner living in the hostel could spend either Saturday or Sunday outside with his family from 0700 hours to 2100 hours every week. In addition to this he could have home leave for 21 days per year, to be taken at weekends. In the last nine months of his stay in a freiganger-heim, a prisoner would be allowed six days per month to be taken at weekends as home leave. The period spent at the freiganger-heim was seen very much as a proving ground prior to release.

Life-sentenced prisoners must have served a minimum of 10 years before being allowed to participate in the freigangerheim scheme. When we visited, one lifer had been on the freiganger- heim for over four years. This approach differed from that of UK prison hostels, where the hostel time would be shorter and the time with family less generous.

Unsurprisingly, we were told that drugs were a problem in German prisons. In the main prison at Bruchsal, if a prisoner was suspected of using drugs or alcohol, he could be urine tested and breathalysed. If he refused to be tested, then his visits would be restricted. If a freiganger refused to be tested he would be returned immediately to the main prison – he therefore had much to lose by refusing.

Our overall impression of Bruchsal was of a high-security prison in which it was possible to use time. We were impressed that, when a prisoner entered the prison at Bruchsal, he did so with a clear idea of what lay ahead; he had his *vollzugsplan* (prisoner's personal plan). The flexibility of treatment, gener- ally achieved in accordance with the vollzugsplan, allowed for a real sense of progress: progress by small, achievable steps. This sense of progress, and knowing what the future held via the voll- zugsplan, seemed to give structure to even the longest sentence. There was no place for the 'dumb' period commonly served in the UK in the middle of a long sentence. There was no need to 'just do time', to just get through that part of the sentence.

It is difficult to imagine tighter security than that which oper- ated at Bruchsal, yet there did not seem to be an oppressive feel about the place. The prison magazine, far and away the most pro- fessional and polished production of its type we had ever seen, was able to criticise the management at both the mildly amusing and the more ferocious levels. We had not experienced this lib- eral approach at home. Bruchsal demonstrated that, even with the highest levels of security, it was possible to have a positive, rehabilitative regime. This was a key lesson for us to take home.

After Germany, we went on to the Netherlands and visited Zutphen and Leeuwarden prisons, two very different establishments, to see how the Dutch prison service, by reputation a forward thinking and liberal service, approached the resettlement of its prisoners.

ZUTPHEN PRISON, THE NETHERLANDS

Zutphen is, by Dutch standards, a very old prison; built in 1889, it is situated about 30 miles to the north of Arnhem. When we visited, it held 96 male prisoners aged between 18 and 35 years of age, all serving sentences of six months and over. Although it is a secure prison, there is no sophisticated security equipment in evidence at Zutphen and the staff are not armed. The prisoners come from all over the Netherlands and beyond; 42% of the population are foreign nationals. Of the 100 or so staff at Zutphen, a proportion were women, and we were interested to know more about the impact of having female officers in a male prison, as women had only recently been permitted to work in male prisons in the UK. When we asked about this, we were told that they had both a positive and a negative effect on the establishment. On the one hand they were seen as a normalising influence within the establishment, reducing the macho image of an all-male environment, thereby benefitting both the male staff and the prisoners. Conversely, we were told, their presence did cause some problems at times, with some young prisoners becoming infatuated by the female members of staff. On balance, the governor told us, the positive effects of having female staff far outweighed any possible disruptive effects. Almost 30 years later, such a discussion feels very dated, with 'cross-sex postings' enshrined in law here as well as being embedded in prison culture.

Many officers had a dual role to play at Zutphen; not only were they disciplinary officers, they were also workshop instructors. This created a unity of purpose with regard to the overall training of the prisoners. Because of the high percentage of foreign national prisoners, staff were also trained to understand different cultures, thus creating better understanding between the staff and their charges. This diversity training would be embraced by the UK Prison Service soon afterwards, and continues to the present day.

The physical layout of the prison consisted of three wings, the induction wing having 10 places and the two other equal wings making up the main part of the prison. Single cells were much larger than those in the UK, although the furnishing was basic. Unlike UK prisons at that time, TVs were allowed in each cell and had to be rented from the prison.

We saw the induction wing, where all new arrivals were located for their first two weeks at Zutphen. An induction programme explained the rules and the opportunities available. During the induction programme there were face-to-face interviews, group discussions and presentations, including very skilled use of video presentations. This culminated in an assessment of the prisoner's training needs and aspirations. The induction period was skilfully structured, intensive, and set the tone for the rest of the sentence at Zutphen. It was superior to anything we had seen in our own service and, possibly, as good as any induction programme delivered in UK prisons in 2017. The regime for the main prison was strict, but positive. Prisoners worked for four hours in the morning, starting at 0800, followed by a 45-minute lunch break. Most prisoners also worked in the afternoon until 1530 but some participated in education classes or sporting events in the afternoon. This working day was longer than the regimes in our prisons delivered, and it was delivered consistently, with work rarely, if ever, being cancelled. Between 1530 and 1630 there was a social hour, which could be used for bathing, visiting the library and general association. The evening meal was eaten in the cell at 1700 hours. Association was allowed for all prisoners each evening, sport being the main activity. One evening each week was devoted to hobby activities and another to a visit from half a dozen people from the local community. These 'worthy' citizens were seen as setting a general good example, and showed the way in which the prison was viewed as part of the local community. Prisoners were locked up at 2130, an hour and a half later than even the most liberal UK prison regime would support.

Each prisoner was paid on average about £16 per week, considerably more than prisoners could earn in the UK at that time. Half of that was required to be put towards compulsory savings, (or sent out to relations), with the rest allowed in possession. The majority of this money was used by prisoners to make telephone calls; these could be made in the evening and prisoners were made aware that staff had the facilities to listen in and even tape the conversations as security required. These arrangements were introduced in UK prisons when telephones were installed and continue to the present day, with the level of monitoring reflecting each prisoner's security category. As we had seen in Germany, maintaining contact with the prisoner's family was seen as being of great importance in the Netherlands, and the visiting allowance was generous. There was a large visiting room for general visits similar to those found in closed prisons at home, plus two private rooms for conjugal visits; again, these were viewed as acceptable in a way that the UK service is still unable to contemplate. Visitors were encouraged to use condoms, either brought with them or purchased by the prisoner from the visits canteen. At the end of visits, prisoners could be strip searched, or subjected to urine testing and breathalysing, as part of a move to combat drug and alcohol trafficking and abuse.

The availability and quality of educational and training opportunities was, again, impressive and superior to that on offer in other than the very best of our own prisons. Also impressive was the recognition of the fact that many of the prisoners had serious personal problems, for example drug addictions, broken homes, inabilities to form stable relationships and selfish anti-authority attitudes. It was recognised that the value to such prisoners of education and trade training was considerably lessened without also working to address some of these other problems. To this end, a number of probation staff, social workers, psychologists and ministers of religion worked in the prison and played an active part in group therapy work and general group discussions. At the end of each year at Zutphen, each prisoner's progress in all areas was evaluated and an individual training plan set for the next year. These evaluations informed the decision as to how, and where, a prisoner should finish his sentence. During the last year of a prisoner's sentence, home leave was allowed on two occasions, and for those whose progress was good, there was an opportunity to transfer to a small open prison, some 15km from Zutphen, for the final few months of their sentence.

At Zutphen, we were impressed by the excellent and searching induction programme and the formulation of a meaningful sentence plan. The annual reviews of the plan, for all prisoners, ensured that the plan was still relevant and had continuing utility as the sentence continued. This was better than anything we had seen before and worthy of consideration in our own service.

Again, we were seeing how valuable telephone calls were to enable prisoners and their loved ones to keep in touch and we were encouraged that this initiative was now being introduced in our own prison estate.

Then, on to LEEUWARDEN PRISON, some 155km north of Zutphen, one of six new prisons built in the Netherlands to replace some of its older institutions. Opened in March 1989, it had 252 prisoners at the time of our visit and was considered to be a large prison by Dutch standards. Of the 252 available places, 72 were for prisoners serving up to six months, 72 for long-term prisoners not considered to be dangerous or disruptive, 96 for long-term prisoners who are considered to be high security risks, and 12 places were identified for extremely dangerous prisoners. When we visited, we learned that it was planned to move this last group of highly dangerous prisoners around other long-term prisons on a 'carousel' system, as part of a new policy. For the 72 short-termers and those 72 long-termers not considered dangerous, the regime was very relaxed with a large amount of time spent in free association. For the 96 high-security prisoners the regime was much more controlled, but still relatively relaxed in comparison to what we were used to at home. This last group of prisoners was made up mainly of hardcore professional criminals, for whom the Dutch prison authorities believed little could effectively be done to change the attitudes and way of life. The policy for such prisoners was to accept 'humane containment' as the best option. The few who did show signs of obtaining any benefit from their imprisonment were able to progress to the more relaxed regime available in the prison.

Reflecting the security category of the prisoners, Leeuwarden had a high level of security itself, consisting of infra-red alarm systems, electronic unlocking systems and cameras. However, no member of staff carried a gun. The design of the prison consisted of one large rectangle surrounding a central open area used for outside association, with one half of the association area being a football pitch with astroturf. All departments, including workshops, were part of the same complex, negating the need for prisoners to move outside of the confines of the building. The wings were of the 'open well' type, with galleries, as in the older English style prisons, with each wing separated from other wings by electronically operated doors. It was interesting to note that this new prison had been built to such a traditional design, whilst, back in the UK at that time, we were designing and building prisons with closed landings and corridors, giving poorer sight lines for staff.

Each wing had three card operated telephones for prisoners' use. All accommodation was in single cells with piped radio and TV. The TV was rented from the prison authorities, just as UK prisons would introduce a few years later. Prisoners had regular access to the canteen, where they could purchase, among other consumables, non-alcoholic beer. Prisoners were paid a reasonable weekly wage; well above the UK levels at that time, with short-termers able to earn about £10 per week and long-termers about £16. Short-term prisoners were allowed one visit each week, whereas long-termers had one visit per month, which could be an unsupervised conjugal visit. The gymnasium was well equipped with keep fit equipment, weightlifting equipment and so forth, which, with the excellent astroturf area, ensured that the physical fitness of prisoners was well catered for. Three priests worked in the prison, but, surprisingly, there was no church there so a small room had been converted into a makeshift one. The workshops, which included printing and carpentry, were used for production and training, with the majority of prisoners working only in the mornings, occupying themselves in leisure pursuits in the afternoon.

Because all of the facilities at Leeuwarden were housed in the one rectangular complex, the first thing we noticed on entering was the sheer size of the place, especially when first encountering the wide central corridor along which all activities were structured. As the prison had only been open a few months when we visited, it felt very modern, clean and tidy. Although it was large, some areas appeared almost cosy, due to the clever use of colour schemes, unheard of at that time in our prisons. Although the facilities of the prison were excellent and the regime relaxed, the prisoners we saw were stereotypical, hardcore, long-term prisoners; anti-authority, arrogant and, we were told, disruptive – the type who push staff and authorities to the limit at every opportunity. One month after the opening of the prison, prisoners in one of the wings had rioted and caused a great deal of damage. The reason for this violent protest was that the colour TVs in the cells were too small!

Leeuwarden was the most modern prison we encountered on our travels and the design had many advantages. The panopticon design of the wings, radiating from an electronic control centre, seemed to marry the best of old Victorian design with the best of modern technology. The cells were almost bedsits, and were as cleverly designed as a caravan interior. The toilet, which was integral, was effectively screened and separated from the rest of the cell: it was there when needed, but was not intrusive, visually or olfactorily, when not required. This was not the design adopted when integral sanitation was installed in most UK prisons in the early 1990s. Instead, toilets were placed in cells, with no screening, so that prisoners had to eat their meals alongside the lavatory.

Next, we flew to Hungary, where our first stop was SZEGED STAR PRISON, HUNGARY, situated 185 kilometres south of Budapest, not far from the border with what was then Yugoslavia. Built in the late 19th century for 500 prisoners, at the time of our visit and after some additions to the original prison, it housed 1,100 prisoners in overcrowded conditions. All of the prisoners at Szeged were serving sentences of five years and over, including life sentences. Unlike lifers in UK prisons, who move prison several times as they progress, the lifers were likely to serve almost all of their sentence at Szeged.

Security was very high and much in evidence. We were conscious of this wherever we moved in the prison. The prison was built to the open wing 'Pennsylvania' design, and observation and control throughout were excellent. From one central point, three wings could be observed. At this centre point, level with each landing, was a control position, from which an officer was able to control the movement of prisoners. All cell doors were electronically operated from these central control points and a large red light above each cell door was illuminated when any cell was unlocked. Staff working in close proximity to prisoners carried handcuffs, a stick (much larger and much more obvious than those carried in the UK) and a tear gas canister, although staff in contact with prisoners did not carry firearms. Cameras were strategically positioned both inside and outside the prison. There were towers at intervals around the perimeter and at other positions within the prison grounds. These were manned by officers, including female officers, with sub-machine guns. We were told that, if a prisoner were to try to escape over the wall and did not stop after being given a single warning, he would 'take the consequences'. An alarm system, based on short wave radio, was positioned five feet from the perimeter wall.

At Szeged, prisoners' clothing contained absolutely no metal whatsoever and each prisoner had to pass through a metal detector on his return from a workshop. The portal detectors were extremely finely tuned, to ensure that no metal at all could get through. All prisoners were required to wear a distinctive uniform (personal variations were not in evidence). Staff, including the governor, wore a very smart uniform and appeared to our eyes to be militaristic and formal in the way they carried out their duties. Dogs were not used.

We were shown into cells that we picked at random. They were very different to anything we had seen at home, or in any of the prisons we had already visited on this trip. Cells were three or four times larger than a single cell in the UK, but were very cramped due to the number of occupants, with 12 to 15 prisoners typically in one cell. The beds were three-tier bunks, having a mattress, pillow and bed-board, the absence of any springing whatsoever making them extremely uncomfortable. In the corner, with a waist-high screen, was a flush toilet. All blankets were neatly boxed at the foot of each bed and basic toiletries laid out on top of small wooden lockers. No personal items, such as photographs, were in evidence. The walls were plain, having no picture board on which to pin personal items such as photographs. There was one notice on the wall depicting how each bed should be made up and the required layout of toiletries. Surprisingly, there was a TV set in each cell, but we learned that these black and white sets could not receive the national stations. Instead staff recorded films and television programmes, which were then piped into the cells from a small 'studio' in the prison. Educational material was also piped through these sets, which could not be controlled by the prisoners.

At the time of our visit, Hungarian law required that, on release, all prisoners should be able to work normally outside prison and, to this end, a strong emphasis was placed on education. In Szeged there were 21 teachers who had also been trained in reform and, therefore, doubled as social workers. After conviction, a complete assessment was made on each prisoner, which included his previous lifestyle and degree of education. These educational assessments, and the sentence plan that followed, aimed to identify and, hopefully, rectify any identified shortcomings. If a prisoner was assessed as below the basic level of education then he had to attend classes, in his own time, after work. The subjects covered included geography, physics, mathematics and the history of Hungary. Leisure pursuits were limited, but there was a well-stocked library and a reasonably large hall with a colour TV where video films were shown at weekends. This hall was also used by the prison music group. There was no gymnasium or weight training equipment, although there was an outside court used for volleyball.

Szeged had its own hospital run by a full-time doctor. The doctor told us that all prisoners were compulsorily tested for AIDS/HIV upon reception. The busiest area of the hospital appeared to be the dental department. Evidently tooth decay was, at that time, something of a national problem in Hungary and attempts were being made to address this amongst the prison population. It appeared that, in many cases, extraction was the only answer, as we saw several rows of dentures at various stages of manufacture.

Contact with the outside world seemed to us to be limited. Newspapers were allowed, but had to be purchased by the prisoners. There was no restriction on the number of letters that could be written but prisoners had to pay the postage themselves. Visits were restricted to one hour every two months.

The governor described to us the work regime for prisoners. He told us that every prisoner had to work eight hours daily, Monday to Friday. The majority, we heard, worked in the furniture shop, which made furniture for sale nationwide, and also from a shop that abutted the prison wall. The furniture we saw was of good commercial quality, was reasonably priced and of a suitable size for flats. It was possible for prisoners to obtain qualifications in carpentry and other trades. The prisoners worked a shift system; those on the early shift were unlocked at 0400 hours and started work at 0520 hours. At first glance the pay for this work seemed very generous, being just below the national average for similar work outside prison, but, in Hungarian prisons, prisoners were required to fully meet all of their responsibilities in respect of their families, and to pay court-ordered restitution to their victims. Clearly, imprisonment was not cheap for the Hungarian prisoner.

Overall, there was a pervasive sense of order about Szeged Star prison, and a clearly delineated hierarchy within the prison. Relationships between staff and prisoners, and between staff members, seemed highly formalised with everyone aware of his or her place in the organisation. There was a real sense of purpose centred upon the work ethic. Material conditions for inmates were basic. In particular, cell accommodation was very over-crowded and was kept bearable only by the application of strict, austere hygiene regulations. It was interesting that, although the fabric of the prison was over 100 years old, imaginative use of simple electronic unlocking had greatly increased staff control and safety.

Only a few hundred yards from Szeged Star Prison was SZEGED INTERMEDIATE PRISON, and it was here we went next. The intermediate prison was a much smaller establishment that held 260 prisoners when we visited. Prisoners sentenced to five years imprisonment and over were required to spend a minimum of six months in this prison before their release, although we learned that many prisoners spent up to two years in the intermediate prison. We were told that this prison was the only one of its kind in Hungary, and that its aim was to combat institutionalisation and to prepare prisoners for release. The rules here were more relaxed, more responsibility was given to prisoners and many of them were allowed to work outside the prison. Visits were more generous than in the Star prison, with prisoners allowed two hours every month, with 14 days home leave in the last six months.

The accommodation in the intermediate prison was in sharp contrast to that in the main prison. This prison was split up into several units, with six prisoners sleeping in each dormitory-type room. The rooms were light and airy, with good cupboard space, and there were many plants in evidence in the room. There was one television room for all the prisoners within the prison. There were good toilet and shower facilities and a kitchen where prisoners were able do some cooking. The television was in a good-sized association room and this television, unlike those in Star, could receive national television programmes as well as videos. There was a room in the prison that was put aside for weight training; interestingly the weights we saw were all homemade.

To our great surprise, only three prison officers were on duty at any one time, looking after 260 prisoners. However, the officers had the help of seven trusted prisoners, who were, we were told, elected by their prisoner peers via secret ballots. Whilst this use of prisoners was, inarguably, imaginative and cost effective, we had a concern that the arrangements contravened United Nations Human Rights standards, which state that no prisoner should have authority over other prisoners. As we walked around the prison, it felt orderly and peaceful, if more regimented than we were used to at home. It appeared that, having progressed through the main prison system, prisoners were well motivated to cooperate with the regime in the intermediate prison. Of course, the likely reason for this was the fact that failure to cooperate was likely to result in the prisoner being returned to the main prison.

Our visits to the prisons in the four countries we visited were fascinating and thought provoking. We found the variation of approach that we had expected, and we saw the 'good ideas in action' we had hoped for. Inevitably, the society in which each prison system operated coloured the way it worked and it was illuminating to see differing solutions being sought for similar problems. All of the prisons we visited shared a commitment to preparing prisoners for release. The better models were those where the preparation for release commenced with the conviction and continued throughout the sentence. This was the practice in Sweden, Germany and The Netherlands. The Hungarian system, in common with our own at that time, had a model that only really addressed preparation for release as that release loomed. The day a person enters prison is the day he should start to prepare for release. Preparation is not just about teaching the mechanics of job applications, form filling, self-catering and so forth. Rather, it is about giving the person a real chance of a future free from offending upon release. It is making him capable of being a contributing citizen. The debilitating triumvirate of powerlessness, hopelessness and uselessness must be continuously countered if the experience of imprisonment is to be of benefit to the individual and to the society within which he functions.

In addition to the techniques and philosophies used to make the experience of imprisonment a positive, if not necessarily an enjoyable one, there were some particular areas that we found of interest as we visited establishments.

Reliable, inexpensive technology was being utilised in almost every establishment we visited. Our own prison system would, in time, catch up and technology is now used effectively across the UK prison estate. But, at the time of our visits, these European prisons were impressively forward thinking in the area of technology.

The use of urine testing to combat drug abuse was also some years ahead of prisons at home and we were clear that it was a proportionate and efficient way to address this shared problem.

Integral sanitation was another area in which UK prisons were behind the curve and, despite the reservations regarding prisoners living and eating in a toilet, we did not need to be convinced that the facilities we saw were preferable to the 'slopping out' that was still practice, at that time, in our prisons.

Other good practice we saw was that of full and purposeful work regimes, with relevant and credible training and qualifications and the appropriate pay for the job. In the UK, our prisons continue to suffer from 'regime creep', where staff work patterns, operational emergencies and a general laissez-faire attitude to making things happen on time all impact on the working day for prisoners and reduce the usefulness of work and training to prepare them for release.

We also saw some excellent examples of policies that encouraged and facilitated the maintenance of family ties and communication with the outside world. The commitment to communications displayed by the Swedish prison service was particularly impressive. Through the use of private visits, telephones, letters and frequent home leaves, the family unit could be maintained. Similarly, in Hungary, while visits were few and short, prisoners did retain a real link with their family as they worked to maintain them financially.

The opportunity to visit prisons abroad so early in my career allowed me to apply what I had seen and learned to my experiences as I moved to work in other prisons. It also showed me that no prison system gets it all right, that there are always things that could be improved, but, equally, there is real value in sharing practice and that collaboration beats competition in running effective prison systems.

6

Shit on the Sheets

After almost four years at Leyhill, I was posted to Bristol Prison: 20 miles, and 100 years away from the liberal and progressive ethos I'd been used to in the open estate.

Bristol Prison was built in 1883 to a traditional Victorian prison design and expanded in the late 20th century with additional accommodation and facilities for prisoners. It was a very typical, unremarkable, local prison, which served the courts of Bristol and much of the South West of England. If you've seen *Porridge*, you'll know what it's like.

Having been a specialist (lifer) governor who could wander around in the sunshine at Leyhill, I now found myself as a wing governor behind a big wall at Bristol. Here, the regime was not based on interaction between staff and prisoners, but was run like clockwork, with little room for discussion or negotiation. Admittedly, to some extent, it had to be like that, to allow the daily complexities of a local prison to work. But this came at a cost, a loss of staff awareness, or at least my awareness, of what was actually happening in the prison.

Prisoners in local prisons are locked up for many hours each day. At Bristol, this meant that they were locked into a space about the size of the average family bathroom. In that space, they would sleep, eat, defecate, recreate and look at the walls for hour after hour, day after day and, sometimes, year after year. In overcrowded prisons, such as Bristol, this family-bathroom-sized cell, designed by the Victorians for one prisoner, was shared with another prisoner who would sleep, eat, defecate, recreate and look at the same walls.

Such was life for hundreds of men in HMP Bristol, as it was for thousands of men in other prisons across the country. If the cellmates got on, it was about bearable. Not bearable in the way that the average man in the street would understand the concept, but bearable as understood by a prisoner.

Can you imagine how many points of disagreement and areas of non-compatibility arise when you're forced to live, cheek by jowl, with a stranger?

As a junior governor grade, one of my duties was to take 'governor's applications' on a daily basis. These are the queries and requests of prisoners that cannot be dealt with at officer, or senior officer, levels and which are referred up to the wing governor, in this case me. The prisoner is wheeled in by a principal officer and the wing governor sits behind his desk and dispenses what passes for fairness and redress. It is pretty mundane stuff.

One unremarkable day, I was taking governor's applications and a young man, aged about 22 at a guess, was wheeled in. His application was unremarkable, as was he. His request was for a change of cell, as he didn't like sharing with his cellmate. He asked if he could move to a single cell. I told him he couldn't, as we, as many other prisons, required 'doubling', that is two men sharing a cell that the Victorians had designed and built for one man. Overcrowding in the prison system meant that the practice of doubling was/is systemic.

He became visibly upset, but not aggressive, and began to plead. The answer was still 'No'. Some prisoners, when they hear

'No', become aggressive and angry and I was used to that behaviour. This young man just looked defeated and sad. This caused me to enquire a little more as to what the problem was. He was reluctant to tell me, but I persevered and, reluctantly and obviously embarrassed, he told me.

He was serving a two-year sentence for car theft. His cellmate was a life-sentenced prisoner, much older than him, in his 50s, who had served a long time on his life sentence, and probably would serve many more years. The fact that the 'lifer' was located in a local prison, and not a training prison, showed that this life-sentenced prisoner was not moving smoothly through the system to a future release date. So this 22-year-old man, serving a two-year sentence, was locked in a very small space with this much older lifer who had no foreseeable release date. At some point, the lifer had made sexual advances to him, which he had rebuffed. The lifer was persistent and was, persistently, rebuffed. The lifer did not become violent but was consistently importunate. And so, locked together, for many hours, days, weeks, this was the reality of this young man's life.

He had slowly become aware that, when he was asleep, the lifer would come onto his bed and masturbate (not his word) over him while he watched him sleeping, and that this happened night after night. If he was asleep, I asked him, how did he know this?

He said, and I wished I hadn't asked, 'He leaves shit marks on my sheets, and cum stains on my t-shirt.' The fact that this was what life was like for this young man, night after night, stopped me in my tracks. It was a glimpse into the private hell, and variations thereof, which did/do take place behind closed doors in many cells, in many overcrowded prisons. I couldn't begin to imagine his misery when, each night, every night, when he was asleep, and unable to rebuff the advances of his cellmate, he was subjected to this. That each morning, when he woke up, well, shit stains don't lie, and semen stains don't either.

I was at a loss to know what to do, but I was unwilling to leave him in that cell. So I did the only thing I could and arranged for him to move to another cell, and share with a different prisoner. God knows what the new cellmate was like. You can hope, but you don't know. When the cell door slams, even the most professional prison officer doesn't have a clue what really goes on. I know that I didn't.

7

Been on Nights?

To allow the Prison Service to tick over 24 hours a day, 365 days a year, a complex pattern of attendance is in place to ensure the right number of suitably qualified staff are in the right place at the right time. The system works, despite unforeseeable incidents and events that could, but generally do not, compromise the system.

Local prison staff become institutionalised and, if left to their own devices for too long, they can start to operate on autopilot. Whilst every day in a local prison is different (who knows who the courts will send our way), in almost every other way each day is the same. If you work in this system for a while, you can stop noticing things.

One day, leaving the prison, I was in the gatelock, there to ensure that sliding doors on the gaol side and those on the outside respectively were never open together. Time in the gatelock is like time in a lift; a minute or two confined in a small space with others whom you might not know. That day, I was doing that time-honoured thing of studying the wall, when one of the prison officers in there said to another, 'Haven't seen you for a while. Have you been on nights?'

There was a pause. 'No, I transferred to Exeter prison three years ago. I've just been part of a prisoner escort, bringing one from there to here.'

There was another pause. 'Thought I hadn't seen you for a while.'

Routine might be essential, but it seldom sharpens awareness.

8

Nowhere Else to Go

Escapes in the 1980s were not rare events; there were dozens a year. True, they were almost always from lower security prisons, but still, they were embarrassing. With much effort, and attention to detail, the Prison Service improved its performance. We targeted our resources and beefed up physical security and escape became much more difficult for prisoners.

However, with the decrease in escapes, a decrease in the *possibility* of escape, there was a marked increase in hostage incidents and rooftop protests. Like hydraulic theory, if you push the pressure down in one area, it will find somewhere else to pop up.

Both hostage-taking incidents and incidents at height are dangerous. Hostage incidents, where a prisoner, or prisoners, hold a victim, prisoner or staff, against their will are particularly dangerous. These incidents often result in physical injury and cause untold stress to all involved. So, having figured out how to stop, or reduce, escapes, we had to focus on these incidents, which required us to develop negotiator training and intervention training as well as incident management for hostage incidents. This didn't stop the incidents but it reduced them and we got better at bringing hostage incidents to a successful close.

We also got better with rooftop incidents. We learned to

canalise and restrict the movement of prisoners when they got access to rooftops and, thereby, limited the potential for prisoners to cause significant damage to roofs. We once again improved the negotiating skills of staff. We improved safety by the deployment of crash mats and air bags, which could, if someone fell off a roof, possibly stop them being killed. We became skilled at the use of cherry picker machines for both negotiation and bringing prisoners down from the roof. Once again, as we got the answers, the number of rooftop incidents decreased but did not stop.

Once, at Bristol, the tall Victorian clock tower in the prison was being repaired and was covered in scaffolding. Two prisoners, who were being escorted past, couldn't resist. Evading their guards, they were up the scaffolding like – well you know. There they stayed for two days and nights with staff deployed at the top of the tower to keep an eye on them. The prisoners were probably not protesting against anything, but, rather, saw a chance for mischief and took it. Staff were posted on an internal ledge to make sure the prisoners did nothing stupid.

As duty governor, I took my turn to climb the metal rungs inside the tower and 'negotiate' with the two prisoners. The negotiation consisted of me saying, 'Stop pratting about and come down'.

'Fuck off', was the response.

After a few hours, they declared that they were 'innocent men', though they could not say this with a straight face. They proclaimed that they had climbed the clock tower to gain publicity for their cases. We looked set for a protracted stand-off, then, just as I was about to set off up the tower once again to 'negotiate', I was told that the Duchess of York had given birth to her first child. This was big national news. I duly climbed the ladder and told the prisoners the joyous news of Fergie's delivery.

'Sorry lads, but you're not going to get any publicity now'. I gave it to them straight.

Whether they had just had enough, or whether Fergie's unintended intervention did the trick, I don't know, but, after a lengthy silence, they responded with, 'Alright guv, we'll come down,' which they promptly did.

9

Unstill Places

The 1990 Strangeways Prison riot was a 25-day prison riot and rooftop protest at Strangeways Prison in Manchester, which began on 1st April 1990 in the prison chapel and quickly spread throughout most of the prison. The incident lasted until the final five prisoners came down from the roof on 25th April, making it the longest riot in British penal history. One prisoner died, 147 prison officers and 47 prisoners were injured. Much of the prison was damaged or destroyed, with the cost of repairs reaching £50 million.

The riot sparked a series of disturbances in prisons across the country, resulting in the British government announcing a public inquiry. A team was commissioned, led by Lord Justice Woolf, to establish: what happened during the six most serious riots (at Manchester, Glen Parva in Leicestershire, Dartmoor, Cardiff, Bristol and Pucklechurch, near Bristol); whether these six riots were properly handled, what caused the riots and what should be done to prevent riots of that type happening again.

The Woolf Report, published in 1991, recommended greater clarity of the respective roles of headquarters staff and governors during serious incidents, as well as more delegated authority for governors in managing their prisons, including the management of incidents. In order to achieve this, and to raise its game in the area of incident management, a new unit, the imaginatively named Incident Management Support Unit (IMSU), was established in Prison Service Headquarters. HQ was, at that time, located in Cleland House in Westminster, not far from Lambeth Bridge and almost abutting what would later become the home of MI5 at Thames House.

By 1990, the rank of assistant governor had been renamed 'governor 5', as part of a grade unifying process that was part of a broader service modernisation package. I, as a governor 5, was posted from Bristol Prison to this brand-new unit, IMSU, and a role that gave me an insight into the incidents that happen, and how they are managed, day in, day out, in prisons across England and Wales.

Prisons are not still places. With currently around 82,000 (45,000 when I joined IMSU in 1990) individuals in prison, there are always incidents. With about 130 prisons, many of them overcrowded, each prisoner with their own criminal history, prisons are unlike any other places. Criminality does not stop with imprisonment; sometimes it gets worse. Even the best-run prisons can be unsafe. All prison staff strive to achieve a safe environment, safe in which to work, visit and live. But it is a never-ending struggle. Even a well-run prison is a moment away from chaos. A well-governed prison is not judged by the absence of serious incidents, but by how such incidents are managed.

Prisons are always in one of four states at any time. I have worked in the first three of the four types of prisons. I do not know of any prison that has yet achieved the fourth state. The four are:

1. Chaotic.
2. Controlled.
3. Ordered.
4. Individualised.

It is dangerous to work in a chaotic prison because, generally, staff are not in control. To improve a chaotic prison, the aim is to create a controlled prison. If a chaotic prison is dangerous, a prison that is controlled can be very dangerous because the risk of *losing* control is ever-present. While a controlled prison is a necessary step on from being a chaotic prison, it is unsustainable for any length of time. The next stage is for a prison to become ordered, whereby a prison has an agreed, if implicit, way of working to benefit the interests of all. Ordered prisons operate on a degree of consensus and are, in my experience, the best achievable. Ideally, I would like to have worked in an individualised prison; that is, a prison where the needs of all prisoners, and indeed of all who work in the prison, are addressed or at least acknowledged. Unfortunately, I never did. In an ideal world this type of environment should be achievable but I haven't seen it yet. I have seen very many dedicated people trying very hard to get to that individualised state. Instead, 'ordered' is, probably, the most achievable and is often a great achievement for most prisons.

Is this because of the pervasive selfishness, which seems so marked in the character of those people who find themselves in prison? Possibly. If I had to identify a single – and shared – trait in the average prisoner, it would be 'selfishness', due in part to the struggle to survive but also, perhaps, indicative of a particular mindset that can lead to criminality. (Not that the average citizen outside of prison is in a perpetual state of altruism.)

Because prisons are such volatile places, incidents occur in them daily. All major incidents must be reported and recorded. The following list shows a small sample of what came across my desk in a typical month.

DEATHS

HMP Norwich. A life-sentenced prisoner was discovered hanging in his cell in the healthcare unit. He had used a bed sheet as a ligature and attached it to the window bars.

HMP Winchester. A prisoner was discovered dead in his bed in the healthcare centre; he suffered from epilepsy and appeared to have died during the night.

HMP Bronzefield. A prisoner collapsed in the exercise yard. She was treated locally and escorted to an outside hospital where she was placed on a life support machine. She was later pronounced dead.

ABSCONDS

There was an abscond from *HMP Hewell Grange* when two life-sentenced prisoners were discovered missing from the night-time roll check. The police were notified.

HMP Wealstun. A life-sentenced prisoner was discovered missing during the midday roll check; the police had been notified.

HMP Prescoed. A life-sentenced prisoner failed to return to the establishment following a town visit; he later telephoned to say that he had been involved in an accident. The police however confirmed this to be incorrect.

ASSAULTS

HMP Portland. Two prisoners were involved in a fight in a workshop; one of them sustained head injuries and was treated in an outside hospital.

HMP Altcourse. A prisoner informed staff that both he and his cellmate were sexually assaulted by three other prisoners in their cell; the assailants allegedly searched them internally believing they had hidden drugs.

HMP Cardiff. A life-sentenced prisoner assaulted an officer when he grabbed him, pulled him into his cell and threw him on the bed. Staff intervened and restrained the prisoner. The officer was treated in an outside hospital for a bite to his finger.

HMP Long Lartin. A prisoner assaulted another by stabbing him in the back with a homemade metallic weapon. Staff intervened after they had got into a fight. The injured prisoner sustained an injury to his back and was treated in the healthcare centre; he declined police involvement.

ATTEMPTED ESCAPE

HMP Brixton. A prisoner attempted to escape from escort while in an outside hospital. He was placed on an escort chain but slipped his handcuffs. Staff restrained him and with the assistance of a police officer, he was returned to the establishment.

BOMB THREAT/EXPLOSIONS

HMP Woodhill. The police informed the establishment that they had received an anonymous phone call. The caller indicated that a bomb would be detonated if a certain prisoner was not released from the prison. Search teams were activated and a dog support team was deployed; nothing was found.

HMP Hollesley Bay. An anonymous telephone call was made to the establishment indicating that there was a bomb. The police were notified and a search was undertaken but nothing was found.

HMYOI Aylesbury. A note was pushed under a wing office door indicating that a bomb had been planted in the room. The room was searched and a box was found. The box contained an assortment of unconnected wires; it was not an explosive device. The rest of the wing was searched but nothing was found.

INCIDENT AT HEIGHT

HMP Wetherby. A prisoner smashed a window, climbed through it and gained access to the roof. He made his way to the boiler house roof and protested about being on a basic regime. He surrendered an hour later following negotiations. He sustained minor injuries to his hands and was treated by medical staff.

HMYOI Ashfield. A prisoner climbed onto a ledge on a unit and refused to come down. He demanded that breakfast should be served again. National resources were deployed, he was removed from the ledge by control and restraint staff, five-and-a-half hours after he had gone up there.

HMP Risley. A prisoner gained access to a window ledge from the enclosed segregation unit exercise yard. He stayed there for six-and-a-half hours before he surrendered.

CONCERTED INDISCIPLINE

HMP Garth. A prisoner was assaulted by nine other prisoners in the residential unit. He was stabbed in the neck with a bladed weapon and was treated in an outside hospital. The nine prisoners went on to damage property and to behave violently, forcing staff to retreat. The Gold Command Suite, which manages incidents from Prison Service HQ, was opened and national resources deployed. The incident was resolved six-and-a-half hours later after the prisoners surrendered.

KEY/LOCK COMPROMISE

HMP Wandsworth. A member of staff who was on escort duty to an outside hospital realised that he was still in possession of a sealed pouch that contained a cell key. The establishment was contacted and the key was later returned. The seal was intact and the key was kept in the safe.

HMP Blakenhurst. A member of staff accidentally took a padlock key home and the lock had to be replaced.

HMP Littlehey. A set of prison keys was discovered missing from the key safe; a member of staff was contacted at home and the keys were returned.

ESCAPE

HMP Rye Hill. A prisoner feigned self-harm with a ligature around his neck whilst he was being transported to another establishment. He pushed past staff when they attempted to cut him down and made good his escape.

HMP Liverpool. A prisoner who was admitted to an outside hospital with chest pains slipped his cuffs and escaped. Staff gave chase but there was a car waiting outside the building and he made his getaway.

While on escort a prisoner jumped the dock at Stockport Magistrates Court and escaped. He was chased by private escort staff and recaptured outside the Court building by the police, 35 minutes later.

While on escort from *HMP Hull* to a hospital, a prisoner requested to use the toilet. An escort chain was applied and a member of staff later felt a tug on the chain. When the toilet door was opened, the prisoner had cut through the chain and escaped through the window. A search of the area failed to locate him and the police were informed.

FIRE

HMP Peterborough. A prisoner set fire to her mattress in her cell in the healthcare centre. The Fire Brigade attended; there was minor damage to the cell. The prisoner, who suffered from asthma, was treated in an outside hospital.

HMP Durham. A prisoner set fire to his cell on a landing. Staff removed him from the cell and extinguished the fire and he was treated by a nurse. Two members of staff were treated in an outside hospital for smoke inhalation.

FIREARMS

HMP Featherstone. A prisoner set off a homemade incendiary device in a workshop; there was no damage.

HOSTAGE

HMP Durham. A prisoner took his cellmate hostage and threatened to harm him with a fork. The victim sustained a laceration near the eye. The incident was resolved one-and-a-half hours later by staff intervention.

HMP Wayland. Two prisoners held another prisoner hostage in a cell. The Gold Command Suite was opened. The incident was resolved by negotiation five hours later when both prisoners surrendered.

HMP Brixton. A prisoner took another prisoner hostage and held a plastic knife to his throat. The incident was resolved ten minutes later following negotiation. The victim was treated by the prison doctor for superficial cuts to his throat.

TOOL LOSS

HMP Winchester. A four-inch flat-headed screwdriver was discovered missing from a workshop; prisoners within the workshop were searched but it was not located.

HMP Manchester. A pair of scissors was discovered missing from a wing office; a thorough search failed to locate them.

SELF-HARM

HMP Manchester. A prisoner jumped from the upper landing of a wing onto safety netting and sustained back injuries; he was treated in an outside hospital.

LOCKDOWN SEARCH

HMP Stocken. Intelligence indicated that a large quantity of drugs, about 500lbs, and a knife were located within the establishment. A full lockdown search was activated but nothing was found.

MISCELLANEOUS

HMP Pentonville. A black holdall was discovered inside the perimeter wall during a routine patrol. The holdall contained a hydraulic door jack, wire cutters and a rope. A detailed map of an escape route was also discovered. The escape equipment was sent for forensic testing.

HMP Belmarsh. Staff discovered a crude circuit diagram and a dismantled alarm clock in a prisoner's cell. The cell was sealed and searched by both ammunition and explosives and dedicated search team dogs. A telephone SIM card was found in the cell.

This was a snapshot of my time in IMSU, but I have no doubt that colleagues today face similar incidents with the same regularity.

10

Suicide and Self-Harm

Prisons have no choice in whom they accept. Throughout my career, I met many people in prison who should not have been there. That is not to say that they had not committed criminal acts, but rather that the solution, in their case, should not have been imprisonment, but treatment. In reality, there are not enough treatment options or beds (they are expensive), and so prison becomes the place of last resort.

Prison governors keep in custody those committed by the courts, and have only limited involvement in the judicial decision-making process. Judges and magistrates, those who take the decision to impose a prison sentence, do, very occasionally, visit prisons, but, in truth, these visits provide limited insight into the reality of prison conditions, and the impact of imprisonment on those held therein. Such visits are normally guided tours followed by tea and biscuits in the boardroom. Judges and magistrates are, invariably, shocked by the reality of prison life, but seem to forget quite quickly as they return to their benches. In fairness, they can only use the options available to them when they sentence and, if the only places available are in prison, and there is a need to protect the public, then prison it is.

Prisons hold many people who are in deep despair. Sadly, these despairing people cannot always see their way out of the depths and so self-harm, or even suicide, is common. You can do everything in your power to try to stop people harming themselves, but it can still go wrong. However, if you *don't* do everything right, it will *definitely* go wrong. It would be difficult to overstate the impact that deaths in custody have upon all involved, not only the family and friends of the deceased, but also on prison staff. For every death in custody, numerous lives are saved by the care and vigilance of said staff. As I have already said, I have seen this throughout my service; prison staff intervening to prevent death or incidents of serious self-harm, spending hours talking to a prisoner in crisis and successfully showing him a way forward. But, it is only deaths in prison that make headline news.

When someone kills themselves in custody, there are investigations; by the police, the coroner, the prisons ombudsman and other interested groups. They all operate with perfect 20/20 hindsight. Too often, conclusions are reached with imperfect comprehension of the reality of prisons.

The Prison Service has a series of procedures that seek to keep those at risk of suicide or self-harm safe. Mostly they work well, but not always. If someone is truly determined to end their own life, it is very difficult to prevent that, and often impossible to recognise the signs of intent. In my 27 years, I saw:

- A man in Bristol Prison who collected his lunch, took it into his cell, ate half of it and then hanged himself.

- A man in Bedford Prison who cut his wrists early one morning when he heard the prison officer coming along the landing, unlocking cells, counting on being discovered and saved. He died of blood loss when the officer was distracted by a telephone ringing and returned to the office to answer it, thereby delaying the opening of his cell, causing him to bleed out.

• A culture of self-harm, at that time, in Brinsford Young Offenders Institution, where young men egged each other on to self-harm, sometimes with fatal consequences.

• A man in Whitemoor Prison who was coming to the end of a long sentence and received a phone call from his partner, ending their relationship, just prior to his release. People in nearby cells said he seemed to be handling it well, but he hanged himself during the night.

• A relatively young life-sentenced prisoner in an open prison who drank a pot of paint in an attempt to kill himself, and who, luckily, brought it back up, and lived.

• Being called to the segregation unit in Whitemoor Prison, on Christmas Day, to see a disturbed man, covered in blood due to slashing his wrists. He said he did it to get out of the prison on Christmas Day; he was taken to hospital to be stitched and he survived.

• A prisoner who had overdosed on drugs in his cell. I was in his cell as the paramedics worked skilfully and tirelessly to revive him. He was saved and, when he regained consciousness, rewarded the paramedics with a string of vile abuse because they had saved him.

• The young man found hanging with one shoe and sock on. He had removed the other shoe and sock, intending to use his big toe to press the cell call bell to bring staff to his cell to save him. He had not allowed for the wooziness upon initially suspending himself, and he died.

• The man who cut both wrists and then jumped onto the anti-suicide wire between landings, spraying fountains of blood everywhere. He survived.

Whenever I took receipt of one of the many reports into a death in custody in a prison where I worked, I always read it in detail. I wanted to see what I/we could have done to have prevented the death, what we could do to prevent future deaths. As a governor, I was desperate for a silver bullet, for someone to reveal that 'if you do this, people won't kill themselves' or 'if you stop doing this, people will stop killing themselves'. But every suicide is the culmination of factors too complex to address successfully each and every day. And besides, to do so would require a level of resources that is, simply, never going to be available.

II

Sex Offenders

There is a hierarchy in prison that operates to the dictum, 'I might be bad, but I'm not as bad as you.' This hierarchy is not about guilt; everyone in prison has been labelled 'guilty' by the courts. It is about shame, or shaming.

Many staff prefer *not* to know what someone is in prison for, so that they can do their job impersonally and not feel any distaste towards the individual prisoner. This wilful 'offence blindness' helps some staff to treat everyone equally. This position is tenable for those staff who do not have to engage in getting prisoners to address their offending behaviour. However, for many staff of all grades there is a need to know the nature of a prisoner's offence(s) in detail. For example, staff engaged in the Sex Offender Treatment Programme (SOTP) do not allow prisoners to minimise their offending but, rather, require them to confront and address it.

The most easily reviled prisoners in most prisons are the sex offenders, the 'nonces', the 'beasts' or the 'bacon' (I've never been sure why this last label is used). In most prisons, most prisoners, as a knee-jerk, revile anyone who is a sex offender. At all of the local prisons I worked at, as soon as a prisoner came into custody, charged with or convicted of offences of a sexual nature, on the advice of their legal advisor, they unfailingly asked to be placed under the protection of Prison Rule 43. Rule 43 was, later, changed to Rule 45 but the impact remained the same.

This rule allowed that certain prisoners be kept apart from other prisoners for their own protection. They would apply for 'The Rule' in reception and I, as the duty governor, would see them and, almost always, approve their being placed on 'The Rule' and kept apart from all prisoners, other than those similarly separated. Most prisoners charged with, or convicted of, sex offences fear that they will face violence from other prisoners, those prisoners who see themselves as 'decent, ordinary criminals' (DOCs), in prison. They are, mostly, right to fear this, as the moral superiority felt by DOCs is pervasive. As with all labels, be it 'DOC' or 'nonce', it conceals as much as it reveals.

For many years, the best the Prison Service could do was to create vulnerable prisoner units (VPUs), where those in danger of violence were kept together, but separate from the general prison population. This allowed the majority of prisoners to vaunt their superiority and vent their spleen on the sex offenders, but kept the latter safe from actual violence.

The hatred of sex offenders runs deep. In Whitemoor, we had, for security reasons, to move a wing of sex offenders to a general wing, and the wingful of integrated prisoners to what had been the sex offenders' wing. The resistance to this move was very strong from the non-sex offenders, who did not want to occupy a wing previously occupied by sex offenders. Amongst the many changes we had to undertake to facilitate this move was to change all the toilet seats in the cells after the sex offenders moved out and before the other prisoners moved in. 'Well, you wouldn't want your DOC bum on a toilet seat previously sat on by a sex offender, would you?' as I was told by more than one man. There have been a few experiments, in a few prisons, to address this 'them and us' culture and to impose integrated regimes. Most, but not all, have ended in failure.

In 1992, I was posted to Littlehey prison, a Category C prison in Cambridgeshire built in 1988 on the site of a former borstal. A former governor had refused to countenance this practice of separating prisoners according to their offences. Many people shook their heads and, reciting the received wisdom, said it would never work. Admittedly, it was touch and go on many occasions and had to be constantly policed, but the practice of mixing up all prisoners did work, eventually.

There were, now and again, prisoners who considered themselves DOCs, who would never consider living as an equal with a sex offender, but these refuseniks were moved on, not the sex offenders. Soon, prisoners realised that they would be disadvantaged if they refused to comply, rather than the sex offenders. Over time, this non-separation by offence became the norm at Littlehey.

In some prisons there are points of contact between, notionally, separated prisoners. So, for example, men of all offence types might attend the same religious service. Even then, the two groups are, routinely, required to sit in different parts of the chapel. This typically allows religious services to be held in peace. I emphasise *typically*.

I always attended Mass in prison, although this did not always bring me the serenity that I hoped for. Whilst at Littlehey, I was attending Mass one day when the priest said, 'Let us offer each other the sign of peace.' This was the cue for the congregation to share handshakes and respond with, 'Peace be with you'.

On this particular day, as a sex offender approached another man, a DOC, and said, 'Peace be with you,' the reply he received was an uppercut, two straight lefts and a kick to the crotch. Staff intervened, Mass resumed and at future Masses, I always made sure I sat with the sex offenders to act, I hoped, as some sort of example to show that everyone should 'play nicely'. These sorts of isolated attacks were, often, about the attacker being grumpy or having a bad day, which he believed could be ameliorated by thumping somebody weaker, preferably a sex offender. Glares and empty verbal threats were, fortunately, more common.

At one particular Mass, there was a notorious prisoner who had been convicted of a high-profile rape and murder and decided to be baptised into the Catholic Church. This was to be done straight after Mass. When the baptism had been completed, the priest turned to the congregation and said, 'I want you all to come forward, embrace this man and wish him love and happiness.'

As the prisoners started to go forward, one by one, to embrace this man and wish him love and happiness, the staff, who were standing around the chapel to supervise the service, looked to me as one and thought, as clearly as if they had shouted it at the top of their voices, 'Wonder what the governor's going to do now'. I would like to say that, in my turn, I went forward and said, to this reviled prisoner, as I embraced him, 'I wish you love and happiness' with all eyes upon me.

But I didn't. What actually happened was that I realised that any credibility I had with some staff and prisoners would be blown, if I were seen embracing this man and wishing him love and happiness. So, I bravely sneaked out of the back of the chapel and had the temerity to bless myself with holy water as I left.

12

Private Prisons Are Wrong

The 1991 Criminal Justice Act introduced competition into offender management services, allowing for the extension of the free market into the running of prisons. HMP Wolds became the first private prison in what would become a 10% share (14 out of 141) of the prison estate, with contracts worth £4bn by 2015 – and counting.

I was, and remain to this day, resolutely opposed to prisons being run for profit. Imprisonment is coercive. People are held against their will in prison, and, if necessary, using physical force. Prison rules state that only the minimum force necessary should be used, for the minimum length of time, which is good, but it is still used to enforce physical compliance. There can be no place for using physical force for profit if the state is to have moral authority.

The private companies bidding to run prisons were new to the world of UK corrections and proceeded to recruit prison governors from the public-sector Prison Service, offering large salaries and material benefits to make the offer of 'jumping ship' appealing. As it happened, the previous governor of Littlehey had been one of the first to 'go over', and it wasn't long after his departure that I received a phone call from a former colleague, an ex-governor, inviting me to dinner with him at a local restaurant, and asking that I consider the invitation 'in confidence'.

I had no intention of ever working for a private company, let alone one running prisons, but my curiosity was piqued and I wanted to hear, from someone I knew, someone who had been in public service, why any private company could possibly think I might be what they were looking for.

The dinner was pleasant enough, and I wasn't paying. I knew the man sitting opposite me and I quite liked him. But the more I heard about profits, bonuses, company cars and other perks, the more convinced I became that I could never work in a prison system where profits were put before people.

The idea of your son or daughter, brother or sister, mum or dad being detained, and possibly physically restrained, by individuals working for a multinational company doesn't sound right, does it? Any society that allows its citizens to be restrained and incarcerated must take responsibility for its actions. If prisons are necessary for the wellbeing of society as whole, then society as a whole has to take responsibility for their running. Of course, it all goes back to the role of the state and public service.

If people didn't get sick then we wouldn't need hospitals, but they do.

If people were innately wise we wouldn't need schools but we do.

If people didn't break the law we wouldn't need prisons, but they do.

Prisons are too important to be run for corporate profit. Rather, prisons should be run by people who have the ability to run them, and a sense of public service. What do I mean by this?

If you believe everything has a price, that everyone has their price, then we're doomed to live in a moral wasteland where those with money thrive and those without suffer; the sick, the poor, the physically and mentally disadvantaged and the imprisoned. If when you see a prisoner you see, not a person, but profit, then you have given up on any concept of living in a compassionate society. Multinational companies making profits out of imprisonment have no interest in social justice and fairness. They disregard the misery present in even the most humanely run prisons. If they could make more money from selling hamburgers than running prisons, they would sell hamburgers instead. It's bottom line stuff and they are only interested in the bottom line.

As for the argument that if private companies can run cheaper prisons than the state, then we should let them, my response is that if public prisons are inefficient, they should be made efficient. It was a disappointing failure of courage and commitment, on the part of politicians and officials, that the public Prison Service allowed prisons for profit to get a foothold. Poor managers, those who lacked the endurance and ability to generate good industrial relations, including some individuals at the top of the service, sold out. They abrogated responsibility and justified their incompetence and lack of ability by saying that 'private companies can do it cheaper'.

In areas of social justice, the state should prevail. It was the failure of responsibility on the part of those at the top of the Prison Service that allowed the profiteers to move in. If indeed prisons were not being run well, then those running them should have been replaced with more able public servants, who should, in turn, have been better managed. Instead what they did was to allow private companies to come in and poach public servants (trained at public expense), to run private prisons for profit; and these were not the best of our people, just those with poor public service ethos and inflated belief in their abilities, or those disappointed by being passed over for promotion. All of them tempted by money.

The savings to the taxpayer were, largely, achieved by paying low rates to private custodial staff, not to the ex-public service managers. Costs were also reduced on the back of the enormous benefit of running modern, purpose-built prisons, with contemporary design in comparison to prisons that had just grown old over time. There are very few old and difficult-to-manage prisons in the private prison estate. When Brixton, a very old prison, was market tested, none of the private companies tendered for it: it was too difficult, and would produce no profit. Somebody has to run the prison at Brixton, but without the potential for profit the private sector wasn't interested.

Running prisons, imprisoning our fellow citizens, using force on them is a reality of our penal system. It is sad that it is necessary, but it is. To do this for profit is neither necessary nor excusable. Profit-making prisons are wrong.

13

Old Places

From 1995 to 1997, I was the deputy governor of Bedford prison. Prisons are full of history, and much of it grim. There are not many prisons on the National Trust list. Of the prisons I served in, the one I found the most fascinating, historically, was Bedford. Bedford is a small town, and Bedford prison sits at the heart of it. John Howard, the notable 18th-century prison reformer, was a major player in Bedford prison and, consequently, influenced the way in which prisoners are treated nationally. He brought humanity into the equation.

If bricks could talk, what tales they would tell of Bedford prison. In the past, most of those who did time at Bedford prison were, as in most prisons, the poor, the downtrodden and the unlucky. Many prisoners were imprisoned for poaching; none, I suspect, for paying their workers wages so low that they had to poach to feed their families. Nevertheless, records show that, as well as the 'usual suspects', Bedford prison has, in its time, held bank managers, magistrates, police officers, clergymen, solicitors, a high court judge and a lord.

The prison was the last recorded site of the execution of a woman in public, when Sarah Dazley was hanged before a throng. There is a woodcut of this event, which shows that it was carried out on the flat roof above the prison gate, so everyone watching could have a good view.

During my time there, a charming Indian man, a leading light in a group allegedly agitating for some insurgency in some part of the Indian sub-continent, was held in Bedford prison without charge for over six years and convicted of no crime before being released to return to his family in Luton.

Within the prison walls, those who had been executed were buried in unhallowed ground. The best-known of these was James Hanratty, the A6 murderer, who was executed in Bedford prison in 1962, though his body was later exhumed. Doubts still remain about his guilt and the possibility of executing an innocent man is only one of the many reasons why capital punishment is, in my view, wrong. If, unlikely as it was, capital punishment had ever been reinstated, I would have left the Prison Service immediately and I know I would not have been alone, with many governors and staff being unable to stomach the abdication of hope that killing another human being in cold blood would entail. There is a mind-numbing circular stupidity to the justification for capital punishment, which goes something like, 'It's wrong to kill, so if you kill, I'll kill you!' The 'Topping Shed' is still there in Bedford but it is used as a storeroom now, the bodies of the executed buried conveniently nearby.

Though Bedford prison has been extended and modified in its 200-year history, the heart of the prison was in the bricks that were laid well before Queen Victoria came to the throne. In the prison attic, there is a row of cells, now disused, which once held debtors and their families, just as in a Dickens novel. These dank cells were heated with a shovel of coal, if the debtor could afford to pay for it, and lit by a lamp, again only if the dweller could afford to pay for it. There was no sanitation. In those cells, debtors and their families existed until 'something turned up'.

Deportation was, often, the best hope of getting out of Bedford prison, as with many other prisons. Most people know of deportation to Australia, but prisoners were also deported to West Africa, if, that is, they didn't die of disease on the journey.

As deputy governor, one of my tasks was to carry out night visits to ensure all was as it should be. My least favourite bit was when the night orderly officer would insist, with thinly disguised glee, that we went along a particular passageway where, when the light was switched on, the floor seemed to come alive: a blanket of huge black cockroaches would disperse and scuttle, slowly and reluctantly, into the drains, only to re-emerge when the light was extinguished. My office was adjacent to this passageway; I tried not to think about my neighbours.

The buildings in Bedford prison were historical but not listed. The only listed part of the site, to my knowledge, was the towering wisteria tree in the inner façade. The wisteria blossomed every year and stayed in blossom for many months. I liked that.

14

Segs

If you want to take the temperature of a prison, the segregation unit is where you stick the thermometer.

You could smell it before you got there. You could often hear it. It was not a nice place to visit, it was not a nice place to work and it was not a nice place to live. As deputy governor, I regularly visited the segregation unit at Whitemoor prison and the smell was human excrement (prisoners smearing it on their cell walls and bodies). The noise was the repeated banging, shouting and screaming from prisoners.

The segregation unit at Whitemoor housed a number of extremely disruptive, dangerous and violent prisoners. The staff working in the unit were routinely 'kitted up' in protective over-alls, helmets and shin pads. Before opening a cell, helmet visors were lowered and strong plastic shields were used to the fore to enter the cell. It was about as bad as a segregation unit could get.

Segregation units are the bottom line of the bottom line – it's where people end up when all else has failed. The staff selected to work in these units must, therefore, be the very best that are available. On no account can those staff working in a segregation unit see themselves as in competition or at war with the prisoners in the unit. There is enough violence and aggression in segregation units without looking for it, or stirring it up, and the best staff know this. It didn't take long in the job for me to realise the importance of de-escalation skills, moderation and decency in staff working in such places. These prison officers were, often, provoked beyond any reasonable person's threshold and yet, still, they treated those in their charge with fairness.

Every time a cell door is opened in a segregation unit, there is a possibility of attack. I soon learned never to stand in front of a cell door as it was opened. I would always stand to the side and wait for any missile or bodily fluids to come flying out before I even thought of turning to stand in front of the door. It is crucial that segregation units are the most closely scrutinised parts of a prison, to ensure the protection of staff from the numerous allegations that are made against them, and to ensure that all prisoners are being treated decently and properly. Standards must prevail.

Many people detained in segregation units should not have been in prison at all. These were, often, men with mental health needs, who should have been in hospital but were refused access because of their aggressive and disruptive behaviour. Instead, they became the responsibility of the Prison Service and, all too often, ended up in the seg. This inability to transfer some individuals to a psychiatric hospital, where an intervention or treatment might have had a positive impact on their behaviour, meant that segregation units held large numbers of people who, to my way of thinking, were 'mad'. What do I mean by this? Those people, for example, who would continuously attempt to self-harm by swallowing springs, batteries or anything else that they could get hold of, those who would try to hang themselves several times a day, or eviscerate (disembowel) themselves, or who would attack any human being who came anywhere near them. These highly troubled, dangerous individuals were left for prison staff to deal with and were found, unfortunately, in large numbers in segregation units, particularly in the high-security estate.

Take Mr P, who was so disruptive that he attacked staff every time they approached him. He was a big man, strong from years of pumping iron in prison gyms (I don't know why we allow them to do that). He had been placed in what was known as a Special Cell, or a bare cell, in a body belt, a strong steel circlet covered in leather secured round his waist, on which there were two D-ring shackles to which his hands were fitted and held, so that they were effectively held handcuffed at the waist and could not be moved up to attack.

I used to see Mr P three times a day. Once in the morning, once at lunchtime and once in the evening, when staff – kitted up – would enter the cell with shields. I would enter behind and talk to him. Typically, our exchange would be along the lines of:

'How are you?'

'Fuck off, you Scotch cunt.'

We would have this same conversation, or variations of it, every day, three times a day. And so the days went on until one morning I went in and found him sitting quietly, on the floor, with his canvas blanket around his shoulders (it is tear proof and cannot be used to hang yourself). 'Good morning,' I said, 'How are you today?'

To my surprise, I did not get the usual tirade of abuse so I left him and went back to my office. Half an hour or so later, sitting at my desk, a thought flashed through my mind, 'How did he get the blanket round his shoulders?' Given that his hands were secured to his side by the body belt, it was, technically, impossible for him to drape the blanket over his shoulders. I hurried back to the segregation unit, spoke with the staff and informed them of my concern, 'He has got out of the body belt.'

The staff entered the cell from behind the shield, still kitted up, and this time he was standing up, still with the blanket round his shoulders. 'How did you get the blanket round your shoulders?' I demanded.

He shrugged the blanket off, exposing himself, (as he refused to wear the clothing that had been provided). He said to the officer facing him with the shield, 'I am not going to attack anybody,' and held out his clenched fists. As he uncurled his fingers, we were presented with the component parts of the D-shackles and the handcuffs. The body belt was still around his waist but he had somehow dismantled the shackles, which he then handed to me. He obviously saw this as some kind of victory because afterwards he calmed down and it was possible to move him out of the Special Cell into a normal segregation unit cell.

Mr R had been at Bedford Prison, and I saw him again a few years later in the segregation unit at Whitemoor. In Bedford, while on remand, he had attacked his cellmate and repeatedly smashed his head against the toilet bowl in the cell, not quite killing him, but coming pretty close. He was about as mentally disturbed as anyone I had seen, and his specialism was to kick the door of his cell in the segregation unit. He kicked it monotonously, continuously, 24 hours a day. It was a drum beat that drove everybody mad. A special foam outer door was fitted to the cell to try to stop it, but the noise still got through. His shoes were taken away from him so that he couldn't do it. He continued to stand at the door with his back against it, kicking, about once every two seconds, continuously, until his feet were a bloody mess. I don't know how staff managed to calm him down, but I know that, for many days, the segregation unit was a place that would have driven anyone mad. Staff bore it well and when, finally, a welcome calm descended on the unit, there was a collective sigh of relief. As well as showing heroic forbearance, staff also pushed for this man to be supported medically and psychiatrically.

As a governor, I never revised my opinion that it was regrettable for segregation units to exist, and especially regrettable that individuals with mental health difficulties were held in them. Society owes a huge debt to those men and women who work in such units.

15

First Command

I did two tours of duty in Prison Service Headquarters; one in incident management and another, a decade later, as head of population management. I felt like a fraud working in HQ, away from what I thought, and still think, of as the 'real' job – working in prisons and dealing with prisoners' lives 'inside'.

During my second period in HQ, and somewhat childishly, I had created a rolling screensaver on my computer that read, *'This is a job but not the real job'*. The then deputy director general of the Prison Service often prowled the corridors of the HQ building (I think he missed the 'real' job too). He saw my screensaver, took pity on me and despatched me to be the governor of Brinsford Young Offenders' Institution just outside Wolverhampton.

I was grateful for the posting and pleased to be a governing governor, back on the prison floor with a job to do. I arrived at Brinsford YOI on my first day and went to the gate lodge. The officer behind the glass took one look at me and said, 'You want next door, mate.'

He pointed me towards another entrance and I went to the other entrance. There was another officer who said, 'Who do you want to see?'

'I don't know,' I replied.

'You're supposed to be the legal eagle and you don't even know who you want to see?'

It dawned on me that both officers had taken me, a man in a suit, to be a solicitor or barrister, attending the prison to see a client on a legal visit. I was mortified to be labelled thus. I made my way back to the gate lodge and explained to the officer who I was. The somewhat embarrassed officer then checked my ID and issued me with my keys. The number on my bunch of keys was 1; the governing governor's keys. I had arrived; I just didn't yet know where.

I took charge of an institution holding 500 young men. 250 of them were, officially, children, aged between 15 and 17, and the other 250 were, officially, young offenders aged between 18 and 21. I also took charge of a dispirited staff struggling to manage the inmate mix, which was, in turn, struggling with itself. I succeeded a governor who had been unwell for some time and who had been moved to a gentler open prison. This was the right thing for him, and the right thing for Brinsford.

In some penal establishments, staff can view themselves as being in competition with prisoners; competition for resources, control and respect. Brinsford, at that time, had this affliction. Staff faced challenge from prisoners, from management and from Prison Service headquarters. They felt misunderstood and unappreciated. They were dealing with what the Youth Justice Board called 'children', but children who might be six feet tall and violent, violent to staff and to each other. Whenever I worked in high-security prisons, I never had any qualms about who I was locking up. Almost all high-security prisoners were a clear threat to the public and deserved to be in prison. Almost all of the young men I locked up in Brinsford were a clear threat to themselves and a bloody nuisance to the public. I met very few young men from a 'nuclear' family of mum, dad and siblings. Most were from 'broken' families with a fluid or non-existent structure. Many came to Brinsford having been brought up in the 'looked after' or care system. Many were closest to the real safety net and unsung heroes of society: grandparents. These children might be six feet tall with a beard, but very few had passed through a caring childhood to get to Brinsford. I struggled with the responsibility.

I struggled with what staff had to put up with, hour after hour, day after day. They were dealing with young men who had no boundaries, had been taught no boundaries by their parents or other adults. Staff were dealing with the constant threat of, or actual, violence. It was not a happy place.

When the deputy director general appointed me, he told me that the chief inspector of prisons would be inspecting Brinsford in the next three months. The inspection had been due at the time of my appointment but the chief inspector had delayed it by three months to give me a chance. The chief inspector's concerns had been heightened by correspondence with the Brinsford Independent Monitoring Board (IMB). This correspondence had stated, in no uncertain terms, that Brinsford was 'not fit for purpose'.

For the next three months, I worked flat out to try to improve what the inspectors would find. I was fortunate to be able to gather a team of high performers. The old top team, tired and dispirited, were, mostly, glad to go elsewhere and those who weren't glad to go elsewhere were given the chance to be part of the recovery. Some were able to rise to the challenge, and those who couldn't were then sent elsewhere. So my new senior management team and I worked flat out to present an establishment that was fit for purpose. It was a disaster.

In retrospect, it would have been sensible to allow the inspectors to come and see Brinsford with all its attendant problems. But it's not in my nature, as a manager, to leave problems unaddressed. So, after I'd done three months' hard work, the chief inspector arrived. I can still recall the pain that I, and almost everyone working at Brinsford, felt when the chief inspector pronounced, in his report, that Brinsford was 'a stain on the Prison Service'. The establishment was pronounced 'not fit for purpose' and a danger to the young people held there. I knew it was bad but the quote 'stain on the Prison Service' was a label that all staff felt as a body blow.

On the day that the inspection report was published, the media interest went into overdrive. After a day of TV, radio and press interviews, all negative, I was punch drunk. I was not alone; every member of staff felt bruised. Later in the day, the director general of the Prison Service phoned me to see how I was. 'I'm still standing', I said, when, in truth, I was sitting down.

So now the real work began. I held a full staff meeting in the chapel and told them that this was not a label that any of us wanted nor merited.

One of the big, visible indicators that we were not getting it right was the number of young men who were self-harming in our custody. There had been a number of suicides at Brinsford. I hoped there would be no more but, within a month of my arrival, there was yet another death in custody. There was a worrying atmosphere of low-level tension in the establishment. Prisoners, children, would taunt staff with threats to kill themselves if they didn't get what they wanted, as adolescent children might do both in and outside prison. It was very wearing on everyone. We had to change things and we did. We didn't just unlock the doors and lock them up again. We interacted with the young offenders, we engaged with them and we challenged, as firmly but as gently as we could, their muddled thinking.

Brinsford was a 'split site' establishment, holding both juvenile prisoners (those aged between 15 and 17) and young offenders (18 to 21). The Youth Justice Board (YJB) insisted that the juvenile prisoners, who were children, be kept completely apart from the young offenders. This theoretically sound principle, when applied rigorously, led to poor use of resources and some avoidable difficulties. One YJB Monitor upbraided staff for putting a child into the same holding cell as a young offender, prior to the two of them being released from custody. In fact, the two were brothers, aged 16 and 19, and were going home to share a bedroom. The YJB Monitor was adamant that they couldn't be in the holding cell together. It's fair to say we rarely saw eye to eye.

It was difficult to get the balance right, because gentleness was, sometimes, mistaken for weakness, but we persevered. I, as did most staff, came from a family that had nurtured me as a child. I therefore could not comprehend how readily these young men resorted to violence, to other young men, to staff and to themselves. But, over time, I came to understand that they behaved in this way to survive in a hostile world.

One of the insults between young men that could not be tolerated was when one told another to, 'Go suck your mum.' When this red line was crossed – shouted from cell windows – it was a prelude to violent fights. I had naively thought that this insult meant that you were childlike and should return to your mother's bosom. A kindly member of staff put me right.

As well as challenging unacceptable behaviour from prisoners, and promoting pro-social modelling from staff, we improved the built environment of the place with no increased resources. Brinsford had been designed by an architect who obviously did not intend to work or live there. Endless drab, bare corridors joined soulless living units. These corridors were disorientating and had the ability to get me lost even when I had been there for months. Where we could, we used uplifting posters and art work to soften the ambience, and inspire the young offenders. The imaginative approach of senior managers and staff was impressive. We introduced a new unit for the reception of young men into custody, which was a point of real vulnerability. We changed the bleak segregation unit into a much gentler induction and support unit, which still addressed the problems, but in a safer way. Most importantly, crucially, we did not stand off from contact and interaction from those in our charge. Almost all staff responded well to this more positive way of working, seeing themselves not in opposition to, or in competition with, those in our charge.

After a year of non-stop challenges, we knew we were getting it right. We knew that the inspectors would come back, sooner rather than later, to see how this 'stain on the Prison Service' was doing. It was still a shock when I received a phone call from my deputy, saying that inspectors had turned up, completely unannounced, and were already at the gate.

'You're kidding!' I said.

'I'm as serious as a heart attack.'

The inspection team, mob handed, were in the prison for over a week. They dug and prodded and sniffed. At the end of the week, the chief inspector came to see me in my office.

'Well,' he said. 'You've shown that no prison can't be turned around.'

This was high praise. But it got better. 'I can tell you that Brinsford is "an establishment transformed" and you should be proud of what has been achieved.'

I was grateful for the new label, but I was left with a feeling of disappointment. In my experience, labels can conceal as much as they reveal. When the inspectorate labelled us 'a stain on the Prison Service', that label had left many staff dispirited and I knew that the new label would hearten many staff. However, I knew that such labels were crude soundbites, seized on by the media, and that, just as we had not been all bad before, we were certainly not all good now. There was still much to be done and what had been accomplished was part of a work in progress.

The next day I held a full staff briefing in the chapel to tell the staff the outcome of the inspection. Staff who had worked so hard, and who had believed that there were better ways to approach our work, were, of course, pleased, while still aware there was much more to do. I, personally, got my own validation not from the very positive press coverage, nor even from warm calls from headquarters. I got my validation from a dour and taciturn officer with whom I had not always had the best of relations. As I walked the corridors, he stopped me and said,

'I used to hate working here but now I enjoy coming to work.'

I had been the governor of Brinsford for 20 months when I received a phone call from the director of high security to ask whether I was interested in becoming the governor of Whitemoor prison, a high-security prison in March, Cambridgeshire. I didn't hesitate.

The truth was, I liked the high-security estate and felt oddly comfortable in that environment. Most of all, I felt no qualms about whoever was being locked up in the high-security estate. I thanked the director of high security for his call, but told him I had given my word to the staff at Brinsford that I would stay in post for at least two years. He asked me when my two years would be up and I told him, 'The end of March 2002.'

'Alright, you'll become governor of Whitemoor on 1st April 2002.'

Fair enough.

I had intended to keep news of my impending departure a secret until much nearer the time. However, the Prison Service is a small world and you can't keep anything quiet, and soon, staff at Whitemoor had told their mates at Brinsford who their new governor was to be. The secret was out. At my final full staff briefing in the chapel, warm words were said on all sides and I was grateful. I knew that we had gone from dull grey to bright grey, and so did the staff.

Being governor of Brinsford was extremely testing. I had grave concerns about who we were locking up and where we were locking them up. Very few of the young people in Brinsford were a threat to society, though many were thorough nuisances to society and a danger to themselves. I worried that incarceration, the negative experiences, would push them from being nuisances to full blown dangers to society.

April 2002 came around before I knew it and it was time to leave Brinsford, knackered and sort of satisfied. I was proud of the staff who worked, with hope, in difficult conditions, often pilloried when something went wrong and seldom praised when they went right. I wished all the locked-up young men well, in hope rather than in expectation. I left a gaol where I worried about those in my charge for a high-security prison where those in my charge worried me.

16

A Bad Day at the Office

At Brinsford, I received a letter that took me back to my time in Bristol in 1990. The editor of *The Prison Service Journal* wanted my recollections of serious prison disturbances during the early 1990s. It gave me cause to reflect. I wanted to know if that level of unrest was a thing of the past. Was Brinsford a better, safer, more decent place in 2000 than Bristol had been in 1990? Had those very difficult events changed things?

In 1990, I was a junior governor grade in a busy local prison, HMP Bristol. HMP Bristol was, as far as I was concerned, an ordered, secure and safe environment that functioned within acceptable limits. In common with many local prisons, it had a long history, and staff and prisoners generally rubbed along well. I liked working there and so did most staff. Most staff and prisoners had developed a mutual understanding that made life acceptable for those who lived and worked there, like a crude form of democracy.

There was ongoing disruption at Strangeways prison and it was a daily talking point. TV and radio were reporting daily and prisoners had some access to both. There was a risk of contagion and we were aware of that. But we knew it could not happen at Bristol, not with our experienced staff, our good control, our good staff/prisoner relationships – or could it?

On the evening of Friday 6th April 1990, the atmosphere in the prison was unremarkable. The next evening, Saturday, I went out to dinner with my wife and returned home to a telephone message asking that I go into the gaol the next day. On that Sunday morning, I entered a prison that was, on first impression, not notably different to the one I had left on Friday evening. I spoke with the deputy governor, who told me that a coachload of prisoners from HMP Dartmoor had arrived the previous night. The prisoners had been decanted and transferred from Dartmoor due to an incident involving concerted indiscipline; in other words, a riot had broken out. On their way from Dartmoor to Bristol, the Dartmoor prisoners had smashed all of the coach windows. The men responsible were now located on A Wing.

Bristol Prison worked, at that time, on mechanical keys, no fancy electronic locking systems. To get from the main gate to A Wing, I had to unlock, and lock, five gates and doors. As I unlocked the last of those five doors, and entered A Wing, which was then the main wing of the prison, I immediately sensed a change in mood. There was a different feel to the place, a feeling of 'tense anticipation'. Something was going to happen. I am not an imaginative soul, but even I could feel it. The Dartmoor prisoners were not known to the Bristol staff, and had arrived in sufficient numbers to have a destabilising effect on the wing, given their temperament. Right now, there was a stand-off between these prisoners and the staff, each waiting to see what the other would do.

Bristol, as with most prisons, had its share of local malcontents who, given half a chance, would cause trouble in an empty house. These few, who did not play the game, were, typically, violent non-compliant men who challenged authority at every turn. The Dartmoor prisoners, supported by our own faction of malcontents, were now becoming very difficult indeed. There were approximately 30 ex-Dartmoor prisoners with an axe to grind about being deprived of their canteen: the ability to buy tobacco, telephone cards, snacks and sweets; the things that make prison life more comfortable and which are highly valued on the inside. They said they had been transferred without a chance to get canteen.

It transpired, as I found out later, that this was not the case, rather, they had spotted an opportunity to get double canteen. I suspected this at the time, but following a number of altercations with staff as prisoners started to promote this fictional grievance, I decided that this was a small concession that could lower the temperature and so I arranged for the canteen to be opened. Despite opening the canteen on a Sunday, and providing the men with an advance (although knowing they were, almost certainly, having us over), the mood didn't ease and there came a host of other demands and threats. Staff were dealing with flare-ups all over the wing.

I could see that staff were working very hard to maintain control of the wings, while a number of prisoners, individually and in groups, were refusing to behave and, in some cases, were being threatening. Staff were talking down groups of angry prisoners. There were scuffles and hard words. Staff were deploying all the skills that we call gaolcraft, to manage the day, but the testing of staff was relentless.

By now, a control and restraint unit – 12 officers armed with helmets, batons, shields and protective clothing – was being kept in reserve, hoping for the best but preparing for the worst. They were stationed out of sight of any prisoners.

Late in the afternoon, I visited the control and restraint team and found them relaxed, bored even, as they sat doing nothing but waiting. 'These things are always 99% boredom and 1% pandemonium', I joked, not knowing that those figures were about to be reversed.

At tea time I ate a sandwich in my office and pushed some paper around.

'General alarm, A Wing'.

My radio buzzed into life. Someone had pressed the alarm bell; it was serious, but, hopefully, not too serious. I took a final bite of my sandwich before making my way to A Wing expecting a difficult but routine event. Instead, stepping through the door, I was greeted by the sight of hooded prisoners throwing whatever they could get their hands on onto the staff below, on the ground floor. *Where did those hoods come from?* I wondered, as they suggested a degree of planning.

A senior officer had been drenched with scalding water, having asked a Dartmoor prisoner to return to his cell. I looked up to see a prisoner I knew, a Bristol prisoner on the 3s landing, shouting 'Help me!'

'Go behind your door', I shouted back and watched him turn on his heels and lock himself up. The next thing we knew, we were being forced off the wing, back through the doors, pushed by the sheer weight of angry prisoners.

I felt sick to my stomach when it quickly became clear that a member of staff was unaccounted for. He had last been seen in a melee of prisoners, as isolated scuffles exploded on every landing. Then came the realisation that this wing was now controlled by prisoners and that those prisoners had keys, having wrested them from a member of staff. I was only very slightly relieved when it was established that the staff member had locked himself in a cell on the ground floor.

An immediate attempt to re-enter the wing was abandoned as staff were met by a deluge of missiles; bins, tables, chairs and jugs of hot water. It was time to go and fire up the control and restraint team, who were, I decided, no longer going to be deployed onto the wing, given that there were 12 of them and about 120 prisoners. Instead, the unit would be deployed to the gated bridge between A Wing and the adjoining wings, B and C Wings, to prevent further spread of unrest.

Or so I hoped.

Having positioned the control and restraint team on the bridge, I made my way back to the outside of A Wing and watched, with a dog handler, as prisoners started to appear on the roof of A Wing. Somehow I felt reassured by the presence of the dog.

As slates took flight (rooftop prisoners showed a quick aptitude for this task), I quickly moved on. It was time to attempt the release of the trapped officer. Staff took up positions under shield-top cover and, using oxyacetylene torches, they attempted to cut the bars of the cell from the outside. Prisoners on the roof were dropping large chunks of masonry onto the shield-top cover, but staff persevered. I shouted to the prisoners on the roof that we weren't trying to enter the wing, but only get someone out; the prisoners were seriously unimpressed by this and gave me the standard lecture on sex and travel, while telling me things about my parents that I hadn't known until then.

A works officer was felled by a large chunk of masonry thrown down onto his helmet and I thought he was dead. He was unconscious and seemed, at first, not to be breathing. He was carried out on a long shield like a knight from the lists, but he made a full recovery in time. Then I was told that some well-intentioned prisoners, local Bristol prisoners, were trying to smuggle the trapped officer, dressed in a prisoner's coat, to the gate of A Wing.

I went to A Wing and opened the door onto the wing, with the control and restraint unit around the doubled, still secured, gate. There was a press of prisoners against the gate, and in the middle of them, the officer, disguised by the friendly prisoners and dressed in prison clothing. Behind the gate, on all levels, was a maelstrom of noise and movement and I thought, 'What if this gate is opened and these are in fact the rioters pressing against it?' It would have been a scrum, we would have lost control and then they would all have been out of the wing and into the grounds.

The gate was opened and about 10 prisoners and one officer came through the gate like a cork from a bottle. The gate was quickly re-secured and doubled. The officer, who had just experienced every member of staff's worst nightmare, was led away to be cared for. The prisoners were relocated to other accommodation, walking, breathing witnesses to good staff/prisoner relationships.

The next job was to get an old and infirm life-sentenced prisoner out of the prison hospital to a place of safety. I knew this man from my time at Leyhill prison and he actually looked pleased to see me. We got him onto a stretcher and, with the C & R unit holding shields above it, got him to safety. While we were carrying him out, prisoners on the roof threw chunks of masonry and tiles down onto us.

There followed a night of mayhem as the rioters tired themselves out. I was with the control and restraint teams as we re-entered A Wing early the next morning, and it seemed like a different planet. Everything had been destroyed. I saw a local prisoner (who had gained access to the pharmacy on the wing), being led docilely away. I found out later that, with access to the pharmacy, prisoners had emptied all the drugs, any drugs, into the wing tea urn and had been drinking mugs of the hot drug brew.

I crossed the bridge from A to B and C Wings with the control and restraint teams. My wizard idea of holding the bridge had been foiled by rioters armed with hammers and other tools that they had obtained from a cell on the wing that was being used as a works store. The rioters had just knocked a hole in the wall above the bridge, and used the top of the bridge as the walkway to get to B and C Wings. I was impressed at this lateral, or vertical, thinking.

I remember the steady behaviour of staff. I had never doubted for a second that we would maintain security and regain control. I felt tired.

Later, I was approached by a psychologist who handed me a questionnaire asking, 'How was it for you?' The sort of thing a holiday rep gives you at the end of your holiday. I was not impressed. I threw it straight in the bin.

The Woolf inquiry was held at a rather posh hotel in Taunton, an incongruous setting, given that prisoners were brought there to give their evidence. I was in the witness box for what seemed like a very long time, and I was probably more nervous than I had been during the disturbance itself. Since then, a decade had passed. I had moved jobs several times, working in three different prisons and headquarters.

In 2000, in the governor's office at Brinsford, I contented myself with asking how my prison, Brinsford, felt – did it feel a just place, a decent place? Yes, I believed it did but then I believed that Bristol in 1990 was also just and decent.

This isn't to say that there aren't always improvements that can be made. Governments decide how much money is allocated to prisons (along with hospitals and schools). There is no shortage of experts who tell us how to do it. Many of them are sincere, caring and wise, while there are others who speak on penal reform with all the experience and insight of Toad of Toad Hall, after he had spent one night in prison before escaping.

It was important that the Prison Service learned from reports such as Woolf's, because these significant events often identify what is wrong and what needs to be different. It is true that 'when reason has resumed its seat' the world can seem a different place. However, to most people who work in prisons, their work is not a theoretical construct but rather a daily exercise in realism and pragmatism. Much of what Woolf recommended has been implemented, and we are the better for it.

There is always a need to assess and reassess but I do know that the vast majority of staff, of all grades, working in prisons, are decent, caring and professional. It was so in Bristol in 1990, it was so at Brinsford in 2000 and, as I write now, safely retired in 2017, I do not doubt that it remains so.

17

Back to High Security

Whitemoor runs through my professional life like the lettering through a stick of rock. I served there three times, as a junior governor grade, as the deputy governor and, finally, as the governor. If you can govern a place like Whitemoor, and not live with a pit of anxiety in your gut, you're definitely missing the point.

Whitemoor holds 400 prisoners, all serving very long sentences for very serious offences. At any one time, over 100 prisoners will be Category A, that is, they are deemed so dangerous to the state, the police or the public that escape must be made impossible: not really difficult, but impossible. A small number of these Category A prisoners are what is known as High-Risk Category A, that is, they have all the combined dangerousness with realistic access to finance and other resources to actively plan an escape.

Normally, the resources means links with, and access to, serious organised crime groups, or access to large sums of money to facilitate escape; sometimes both. When I became governor, there were about 18 of these High-Risk Category A prisoners and a further small group of about six, when I took command, who were deemed to be Exceptional Risk Category A prisoners. These were men with the required level of dangerousness, access to serious organised crime groups or huge sums of money, and for whom there was active intelligence that an escape plan was underway.

In most of the prisons in which I worked, the most complicated electrical device was a lightbulb. This, you'll be relieved to hear, wasn't the case in Whitemoor. Here, electronic devices and fields, added to other physical security devices and systems, meant that, if you were committed here, here you stayed.

Back in the 1990s, however, the prison had been in chaos. Prisoners were unruly and not fully under the control of staff. Assaults were commonplace and, often, serious. Staff felt unsafe and so did most prisoners. Prisoners routinely filled bottles with urine and excrement and threw them high up on a wall, so that, as the bottle smashed, those below were showered with the contents. This meant that, over time, the balance between security and control on the one hand, and allowing prisoners some measure of self-determination within a very secure perimeter on the other, was lost. Consequently, Whitemoor, then, was not a positive place to work. At the end of each working week, before going home, I used to make myself go down onto each wing and walk every landing before going off duty. I did this to stop myself from becoming 'prisoner shy'. It was always a temptation to stay in your office, away from the constant hassle of being harangued as a 'walking suit' on the landings. You had to be able to do the office work and be able to walk the landings. Never easy.

In September 1994, having left Whitemoor only a month or so earlier, I woke up to hear on the radio that six Exceptional Risk prisoners, mostly Provisional IRA prisoners, had managed to escape from the special secure unit. There followed a very detailed enquiry, the Woodcock Report, which established that the weakness in what I, and many others, thought was an impregnable security system was human error. The systems were in place, but people can make mistakes. Staff in the SSU had been conditioned, over time, to respect, and meet, prisoners' needs, including providing them with curtains, behind which they fashioned their escape. Once again, this was due to not getting the balance right. Staff were under-supported and not sufficiently trained to deal with the sophistication and ruthlessness of those in their charge. A series of hard lessons were learned.

When I returned to Whitemoor, in 1996, as deputy governor, the Woodcock recommendations had been implemented and the balance between prisoners' rights and security was about right. This had been achieved through the hard work of staff, led by an effective governor. As the deputy governor, I didn't have the ultimate responsibility but was, mostly, left to run the prison on a day-to-day basis.

The highly complex factors at work in the high-security estate became evident when I had the duty of delivering the 'tariff' to the so-called Balcombe Street Gang. A tariff is the decided minimum time that a life-sentenced prisoner must serve in custody to satisfy the needs of justice, and prior to being considered for release. The Balcombe Street gang were Irish republican prisoners who had caused death and mayhem in England, culminating in an armed siege in Balcombe Street, London, where they had been run to ground by the police. Some years had passed since they had been given their life sentences, but their tariff had not yet been decided. I had been approached by more than one of these men and asked when they would be told how long they would have to serve.

The decision regarding tariff length was made by the Home Office. I was, therefore, surprised to be phoned, personally, by Prison Service Headquarters, and informed that the decision about the Balcombe Street Gang members' tariffs had been made and that I, in the absence of the governor, would have to inform them of that decision. The next day, I received the tariffs and arranged to see each gang member individually to tell each one how long they would have to serve in prison before being considered for release. Each and every one of them had been given a tariff of 'natural life', meaning they would stay in prison until they died. I presumed that this would be a devastating blow and I wasn't looking forward to telling them.

They came into the wing office, where I had chosen to disclose the tariffs, one by one, and I told them, one by one, handing them the decision in writing. Each of them took the paper, smiled, thanked me and left the office. It was not the response I had expected.

The rule is that no life-sentenced prisoner can be considered for transfer to another jurisdiction until they have received their tariff and know how long they must serve. With this issue decided, the gang members' bar to consideration for transfer to the Republic of Ireland had been removed. Within a month or so, all of the Balcombe Street Gang had been transferred from Whitemoor to the Irish Prison Service and within a further month, I saw them on TV, at rallies in Ireland, apparently out on licence. All I can say is that I know that the repatriation of these types of prisoners played a crucial part in the very complex negotiations that led to the – relative – peace that now exists in Northern Ireland. Such decisions were taken way above my pay grade. I left Whitemoor with a greater awareness of the politics at play in the high-security estate.

In 2002, I found myself back at Whitemoor, and this time as the governor. I had no doubt that the people I was locking up *should* be locked up, which made the business of being a gaoler easier. I had no qualms that what I was doing was right and necessary for the protection of the public. I was the beneficiary of years of hard work by dedicated staff and good governors and I was able to continue their legacy during my time as governor of Whitemoor.

Sooner than expected, I got a phone call from Prison Service Headquarters. This time, I was asked to consider putting my name forward for the post of area manager, responsible for all the prisons in the east of the country. I duly applied and was selected to be responsible for the 13 prisons in the Eastern area. I knew I would be busy and that the role would be testing.

Still, it was with real regret that I hung up my keys for the last time as governor of Whitemoor. I knew that the staff at Whitemoor, and the other seven high-security prisons, do an important public service, often in trying conditions and out of public sight. The only time that the public become aware of the job that staff do is when something goes wrong. Staff do not get the credit for all that they do, but have the consolation of knowing that they are doing a tremendous job.

18

Going Sick

The first governor I met in the Prison Service was a man who had worked his way up from being a works officer to the governing governor of a prison. I was in his office talking to him just before he retired, and he was musing about his service. 'The thing that gives me the greatest pride is that in my 30 years of service, I haven't had a single day off sick,' he told me. At the time, I wondered how he could consider this his greatest achievement. Then, new as I was to the Prison Service, it struck me as a somewhat unremarkable fact.

Seventeen years later, I stood in front of several hundred staff in the Whitemoor prison chapel, as the newly appointed Governor, and addressed my first full staff meeting. I spoke to them about something I was intending to focus on, something that I believed was preventing Whitemoor from achieving its real potential: staff sickness levels.

Full staff meetings are, typically, held monthly and give the governor a rare opportunity to gather together all available staff and brief them on important issues, share news, both good and bad and, in this case, talk to them about what I'd found in my first days back in the prison and what my priorities would be as the new governor. In the 17 years since my conversation with that retiring governor, I had come to see that staff sickness is a facet of prison culture; it is something that causes, and exacerbates, many of the operational difficulties prison managers face every day in their prisons.

I do not believe that the Prison Service is unique among public services in having this problem, although I certainly did not experience it during my Army career. Perhaps as a consequence of this, I managed sickness robustly and took what many considered to be a very hard line.

If somebody is so sick that they cannot come to work, and so sick that it's reasonable that somebody else does their work for them while they themselves are still paid, I have no difficulty with that. However, there is an absolute underlying need for people to be clear that they are so sick that they cannot come to work, not just feeling a bit unwell, or simply can't be arsed.

The Prison Service has a bad sick record compared to other public sector areas and an even worse sick record in comparison with the private sector. There is no shortage of theories about why this should be; people talk about the stress of the job, and so forth. I don't buy it. In my opinion, only the breaking of bones or a major illness justifies staying at home.

In my 27 years in the Prison Service, I was never so sick that I was not able to go to work. I was sick on a number of occasions during those 27 years, but never so sick that it was reasonable to expect somebody else to do my work for me while I was still paid.

The job does not go away. It is there 24 hours a day, 365 days of the year, and somebody has to do it. When an individual is so sick that they cannot come to work, then somebody else does their work. I had the usual share of colds, coughs, sniffles, headaches, hangovers, bad backs and so forth. I have been punched in the mouth more than once, but I still came to work. I am not unusual – the majority of prison staff have laudable attendance records.

I know that's tempting fate and I know that people do get so sick that they cannot come to work. I could have had my heart attack or my stroke whilst driving home from work one night, I could have crashed my car or found a lump somewhere it shouldn't be – all the things that can happen to anybody at any time. I do not intend in any way to diminish the reality of disabling sickness for some people and, in the end, for almost all people. However, with a reasonable degree of psychological and physical robustness, it is possible to continue to do your job whilst you have got a sniffle or a sore back or a sore toe or a hangover or you have been punched in the mouth the day before.

Perhaps I should add that I do not always eat the right food, I don't take enough exercise, my wife tells me I am too fond of red wine; in short, I really don't take great care of myself. So I do know that I am a minute away from any of the health catastrophes that can befall anybody, but in all my years working in prisons, I was never so sick that I couldn't do my job.

The robust management of sick absence is a duty that all Prison Service staff owe to the public. Every penny that is spent in the Prison Service is a penny that has been paid in tax by the public. So it's not acceptable to misuse that money in any way or to not properly husband it. Staff are the most expensive part of the Prison Service budget and it's up to everybody to ensure that staff are well looked after and used efficiently.

It is crucial that people who are so sick that they cannot come to work should be supported and cared for. It is equally crucial that people, and there are only a very small minority of them, who misuse and abuse sick absence procedures are dealt with robustly. As a Prison Service governor, I probably spent 95% of the time that I spent on personnel matters dealing with less than 5% of individuals, and the vast majority of our staff just got on with their work and did it to a high standard.

Sick absence management can be tiresome. It can be difficult to look a person in the eye and say 'I know your sickness is genuine, otherwise I would be dealing with your absence under the Code of Discipline. It is clear, though, that you are just not well enough to be able to do this job. There is no shame in that, but if you look at your Sick Absence Record, it shows absence at a level that the job simply can't tolerate. You are just not well enough to do this job – so we must part.'

As I said before, the work does not go away, somebody has to do it, and if you have 10% of your staff sick, then 90% of your staff have to do 100% of your work. One person's sick day is somebody else's shift extension or cancelled rest day. It is reasonable to expect people to apply a rigour and robustness to themselves that allows them to work through minor ailments. I have heard people say, 'Oh, I didn't come to work because I had a cold and I didn't want to spread it,' but I bet it didn't stop them going to the supermarket or picking the kids up from school etc. It's a specious argument.

I know this won't be a popular thing to say, but working in the Prison Service is no more stressful, in my view, than the vast majority of jobs. There are different stresses, so for example somebody working for the Rover Group who has just been made redundant, and had had a period of uncertainty before redundancy, will undoubtedly have been far more stressed than a prison officer on a landing in a well-run gaol. There are different levels of stress in different jobs. The security of tenure in public service, for example, reduces a great deal of the pressure that other people might have, say, working in a private sector company, where your job isn't as secure.

In my opinion, the endless talk of stress is sometimes counter-productive not only for the Prison Service but for the individual. There is a psychological and spiritual hypochondria at play that suggests it's okay to be stressed and go off sick with stress. But with it comes a continuing lowering of the bar to the point where anybody who has a bad day at work, or is faced with a decision that they don't like, or just receives a harsh word or a hard look, feels 'stressed' and goes off work. You might call it the 'medicalisation of dissatisfaction'. With this culture of self-pity comes the deployment of counsellors at the drop of a hat. I sometimes wonder what we did before there were counsellors. Goodness knows how people got through the Blitz without counselling – but they did.

The Prison Service is not unique in offering a range of counselling. The Prison Service staff care and welfare organisation's literature states, *'In recent years the Staff Care and Welfare Service has funded a significant proportion of the counselling offered to staff who have been suffering from a wide range of stress and similar problems.'* It goes on, *'The British Association for Counselling and Psychotherapy is registered and has accredited counsellors who will be used and alternatively, where appropriate, staff will be offered cognitive behavioural therapy and eye-movement desensitisation reprocessing.'*

Sometimes it's hard to keep a straight face!

As for Whitemoor, where staff sickness was running at an unacceptably high level when I arrived back then in 2002, it became one of the best performing prisons in the country with regards to sick absence levels and almost all other relevant indicators of performance by the time I left. This was no accident; we managed sickness robustly, supported staff where appropriate and sanctioned them when we had no choice. It worked, and everyone was the better for that approach.

19

Escape

The core business of the Prison Service is to prevent escape. Its statement of purpose states that it serves the public by *keeping in custody* those committed by the courts. In June 2002, three months into my time as governor of Whitemoor, I received a phone call at home, late one Sunday afternoon, from the deputy director general, informing me that a prisoner had escaped from a large London prison.

'We need you to carry out a swift and full investigation into the escape. This is a real "over the wall" escape,' he told me, 'We need to know how this has happened and how we stop anything like it happening again.'

When a serious incident happened in a prison, an investigation was immediately conducted by someone of appropriate rank from another prison or from headquarters. I had carried out many such investigations, and would continue to do so during my career. The purpose of these investigations was to learn lessons for the future, rather than to apportion blame.

However, on this Sunday in June, my first thought was: who would take charge of Whitemoor in my absence? Then, who would be on my investigation team? And, just as importantly, how would we juggle childcare if I was to be spending time in

London? Nonetheless, I packed my bag and, the next morning, I found myself with the area manager responsible for prisons in London, and received from him my terms of reference. These were, briefly, 'Your investigation should find out what took place, causes, the manner in which it was managed and resolved, and how a similar occurrence might be prevented or avoided in the future. You should specifically enquire into:

(1) how the prisoner escaped;
(2) any remedial steps that had been taken to prevent a recurrence;
(3) whether these were adequate;
(4) whether a risk assessment was conducted on the area of the escape; and
(5) any further areas of vulnerability.'

I was also informed that the report should make recommendations in order to prevent recurrences, specifically related to this prison, but also to the Prison Service in general, and on better handling of incidents in the future.

I quickly identified a small team to help in the investigation. I took someone from Security Group in Headquarters who was particularly savvy with physical security issues. I had a liaison officer from the London area office, and I took my secretary, from my day job as governor of HMP Whitemoor, so that I could produce the report contemporaneously.

Striking while the iron was hot, I went directly to the large London prison in a car, with the area manager from London. Here, we met the governor and the deputy governor, and went to the scene of the escape. In the next five days I intended to produce a report that, hopefully, would be of assistance to the Prison Service and to this prison in particular.

I viewed all of the CCTV footage, then I walked and climbed the escape route. I interviewed a total of 17 prison staff and a

prisoner who had pertinent information. My attempt to interview another prisoner who had been involved in the escape, and
indeed had only *not* escaped through a loss of nerve on his part,
was unsuccessful; his rebuttal of my request to be interviewed
was robust, colourful and to the point.

I was surprised at the layout of this fairly typical, large London
prison, having never been there before. It seemed to have 'grown'
across its site over many decades. It was a pre-Victorian prison,
and work to build it had commenced in about 1822.

A few other facts, then.

The prison held prisoners on remand, those committed for
trial and some convicted prisoners. Overall physical security at
the prison fell well below the standard required for Category B
establishments. It was 'hugger mugger' with the surrounding
houses, the wall was too accessible from both inside and outside
and the average family home would have had more electronic
security. Indeed, the most recent security audit had noted that
the physical security provided in some areas of the establishment
was poor. The same audit had awarded 'unacceptable' ratings to
central elements of the control system such as searching, keys,
locks and gates, the absolute basics of physical security.

The prison was in the throes of major building work, particularly to enhance the healthcare centre and to improve the
activities available to prisoners within the prison. The work
being done on the healthcare centre meant that scaffolding, clad
in galvanised iron (wriggly tin), covered the building. It made me
think, unfondly, of the Bristol clocktower. I quickly established
what had happened.

On Sunday 30th June, Prisoner X was amongst 180 prisoners
from A Wing, who were exercising on the yard between that wing
and the old healthcare centre. The perimeter of the exercise yard
was enclosed by high fencing. The exercise had begun at about
1315 hours. The exercise yard was directly covered by two security

cameras and another camera could be panned round to see the yard. The exercise was overseen by two prison officers positioned outside the exercise yard fence, at either end of the yard. Inside the exercise yard, the wriggly tin covering of the scaffolding on the healthcare centre had a length right along inside the exercise yard on one side. The scaffolding and the cladding quality and construction did not meet the requirements of security.

At about 1557 hours, the staff in the communications room had reported that an alarm within the barbed wire on the top of the visits and gates buildings, abutting the old healthcare building, had been activated. I viewed video footage from one of the cameras that showed Prisoner X climbing onto the roof of the old healthcare centre, via the scaffolding, onto the flat roof above the gate building. The establishment contingency plans were then activated and staff responded to the area of the gate. However, while the staff were responding, Prisoner X descended from the roof of the gate area (where there was no barbed wire), into the road outside the prison and made good his escape. He remained unlawfully at large for many weeks before being recaptured in the Irish Republic.

By reviewing the video footage, and other material, I started to work backward to see how he had been allowed to escape. It had been noted by staff, two weeks prior to the escape, that someone had interfered with the cladding on the exercise yard. The damage was repaired, only for it to be tampered with again. An anonymous note had been put into the postbox on A Wing on 22nd June, reporting prisoner access through the cladding into the old healthcare centre. Following the initial damage to the cladding, a decision had been taken to place an operational support grade (OSG – that's an auxiliary prison officer) behind the cladding in the old healthcare centre when exercise was taking place, so that anyone who interfered with the cladding would be challenged. However, the OSG was only detailed to that post on weekdays, and so was not in place when the escape took place at the weekend.

Prisoner X was due to be tried at Kingston Crown Court. Early in his remand time in prison, he had been submitted as a potential Category A prisoner, but this status was not confirmed. However, his level on the prisoner escort record form, on his receipt into custody, was noted as 'No Known Risk'. He had been received at the prison on the 24th of June, from another London prison, where he had been placed in the segregation unit due to him having allegedly made threats against staff. He had numerous previous convictions, and had served 12 previous prison sentences, although he was only 26 years old. His behaviour in prison had, historically, been very problematic. He was facing current charges of robbery, conspiracy to rob, handling stolen goods and perverting the course of justice. His previous offences, dating from 1987, included two offences against a person, five offences against property, 62 offences of theft and kindred, one offence of public disorder and four offences related to police and courts, and a further 47 miscellaneous offences. His movement around the prison was restricted and he had to wear distinctive clothing with fluorescent patches, to reduce any possible escape activity.

On arrival at the prison, he had been placed on a normal wing, in fact on A Wing, and there had been no security intelligence information on him. I concluded that during the short time between Prisoner X arriving in this prison, and his subsequent escape, it was unlikely that he could have created and implemented his escape plan without the benefit of the reconnaissance and knowledge of others.

I was puzzled as to how an exercise yard covered by three cameras and two officers had facilitated or allowed this escape to take place. I soon discovered that the camera cover in the yard was incomplete with blind spots on both cameras, and in fact only one camera showed the cladding on the scaffolding, and that was only a side-on view. The officer supervising the exercise at one end of the yard would have had a good view of the escape site had the yard been empty, but the yard had not been empty. There were 180 prisoners in the yard and video footage shows that large numbers of prisoners were instrumental in blocking the view of the prison officer at that end of the exercise yard. I formed the view that these prisoners acted in concert. From the start of the exercise until the exercise was terminated, there were always a number of prisoners in front of the officer blocking his view and engaging him in conversation. At the time the escape commenced, there were up to five prisoners at a time blocking his view and engaging him in conversation, including one who stood with his back to the officer. Furthermore, a large number of prisoners, about 15–20, had positioned themselves on the yard so that the scaffold cladding could not be seen by the officer. This also appeared deliberate and orchestrated. The officer at the other end of the exercise yard supervising the exercise had no vision onto the escape site.

I noted from the video that a number of prisoners repeatedly kicked the cladding to make a noise to cover the escape activity, which started with a gap being made in the cladding to allow access to the scaffolding. I had seen prisoners kicking the scaffold cladding at other exercise periods when I had been about the prison during my investigation, and I was told by staff and prisoners that it was done to 'annoy staff'. In fact, it was clear from about the time of the start of the exercise that the prisoners had worked together to create an opening in the scaffold cladding. It is debatable whether this opening in the cladding could have been made without some sort of tool. I formed the opinion that it could just about have been done, but that it would have been very difficult. However, I ascertained that no prisoners had been searched going into the yard, so it is possible a tool of some sort was available to them. Furthermore, prisoners weren't searched as they left the yard, so a tool could conceivably have been taken off. One prisoner, a wheelchair user, could have conveyed any tool on and off the yard, and video footage, while not conclusive, seemed to support this. However, on interview the wheelchair-using prisoner denied it, or any part in the incident. I also noted from the video that prisoners were positioned so that they were watching the camera that could pan across the yard, to spot if it started to do so. At one point when the camera moved to cover the yard, a signal was passed to stop attacking the cladding until the camera had panned on.

At around 1540 hours, Prisoner X and others had created a gap in the cladding and X, and at least one other prisoner, had entered the area behind the cladding and climbed up onto a scaffold platform above them, using an old window grille fitted to the wall as a ladder. Careful viewing of video footage shows first Prisoner X, and then at least one other prisoner, climbing up from ground level and then disappearing from view behind the sheeting covering the building work on the old healthcare centre. As it was a weekend, there was nobody on site and no building activity. They made their way around the building and then, using wooden planks from within the workings inside the healthcare centre, crossed a gap onto the flat roof of the gate house. It was when the scaffold plank that they used to cross onto the gate area touched the barbed wire on the roof that the alarm contained in the wire went off. This was at 1557 hours. There was clear video footage of Prisoner X moving across the plank from the old healthcare centre to the gatehouse roof, running along the area above the gate, running back and seeing that the other prisoner had not followed, due I believe to a loss of nerve (it was a long drop onto concrete below between the two buildings and it would have tested the nerve of anyone to cross this gap on scaffolding planks). Prisoner X, having crossed the gap, then turns, runs towards the gate area, descends to the ground and is seen no more.

The other prisoner who had climbed the scaffolding with him had ample time to retrace his steps and re-emerge onto the exercise yard and mingle with other prisoners until exercise was terminated, at 1606 hours. I identified this other prisoner, but he declined to assist me in my investigation.

In conclusion, I believe that Prisoner X acted in concert with other prisoners, at all stages of the planning and implementation of the escape, and that he was the beneficiary of previous planning by others, and they probably remained at the prison.

A series of actions were undertaken immediately to render the area of the cladding in the healthcare centre secure – shutting the stable door after the horse had bolted.

Once inside the cladding, prisoners were effectively on a building site, and there were large amounts of material that they could, and in this case, did, use to breach the perimeter of the prison. The standards required to secure the prison were not being met. Further, the perimeter wall of the prison was not fully covered by barbed wire, or S-wire.

I then looked at the three elements of security: procedural security, physical security and dynamic security. With regards to procedural security, I found that the prison's security department functioned at a fitful level. Management and staff had to deal with a high level of sick absence. Security staff from top to bottom were disillusioned at what appeared to them to be the low priority afforded to security. The wider picture, however, showed an establishment deploying a coping strategy day by day to ensure that prisoners were treated decently and humanely. The courts had to be served, visits run, exercise given, meals served. Staff were cross-deployed daily to meet the basic needs of the establishment. The establishment had made strenuous efforts to match the staff available to the work needing to be done but the security department was often understaffed. On some days, the security department was effectively reduced to just one officer who worked solely as a collator.

The absence of meaningful risk assessments for the high-risk areas within the establishment and the pressures that managers were under across a spectrum of issues seemed to have created a reactive climate at best.

It is possible that the huge demands being placed on the governor and the staff, for strategic planning and for an in-house bid as part of a market testing of prisons, had forced management and staff to take their eye off the security ball. The prison managers and staff were, essentially, bidding for their own jobs with the possibility of the prison being privatised if their in-house bid was unsuccessful. Further, the establishment was expecting a series of audits in the near future and this, combined with the work on the in-house bid, had consumed all the managerial resources and left none over for security.

It was clear that security was not championed to staff and not routinely policed by managers to ensure that staff knew what they should be doing, and when they should be doing it. So, for example, the exercise yard, which should have been searched before exercise, received, at best, a cursory walk through by an officer who failed to inspect the cladding. One hundred and eighty prisoners had gone onto the yard, with none of them being searched either on or off the yard; this was indicative of an over-relaxed approach to security.

Typically, then, staff seemed to be running at 100 miles an hour to stand still. When I spoke to staff they were unclear why they should check the exercise yard before exercise and what they should be looking for. Indeed, they were also unsure why they should be supervising exercise, and what they should do when they were supervising exercise yards. It was obvious that there was a need for clear, consistent and constant management checks that would ensure that staff knew what they were doing, why they were doing it and that it would be checked that it was being done. There was a need to re-energise the security department. Procedural security, the control and movement of prisoners, was lackadaisical, evidenced by the absence of any searching of prisoners leaving the wing to go onto the exercise yard, or going the other way.

Dynamic security is the interaction between prisoners and staff. I observed good relationships between prisoners and staff on the wings of this prison. However, my concern was the staff-free zones that emerged while exercise was taking place. The two officers outside the wire looked into, but were not in, a yard with 180 prisoners moving about.

While the transient nature of the population in prisons can restrict dynamic security, it is only when staff and prisoners are moving amongst each other that the significant benefits of this type of security can be achieved. It is for managers of all grades to set the tone for dynamic security, by ensuring, for example, that there are no areas of 'no go', whether prisoner-created, or policy-created.

The escape of a prisoner from inside a prison is the worst failure that the Prison Service can experience. There is no doubt in my mind that what happened at this large and fairly typical London prison was due to the pressures of other managerial activity; staff took their eye off the ball and so did managers. Prisoners, on the other hand, have no other imperative. They have 24 hours a day, 365 days a year, to watch, wait and plan. On this occasion, they got it right and we got it wrong. That really hacks me off.

20

Dubrava Prison, Kosovo

In 2006, whilst working as the area manager for prisons in the Eastern Area, I was asked to undertake a review into prisons in Kosovo. At that time, Kosovan prisons were under the control of the United Nations Mission in Kosovo (UNMIK) and I was asked to assess the feasibility of returning the management of Kosovan prisons to Kosovan control. The proposal interested me and so I agreed to go, taking with me a colleague to act as a staff officer and flying out a few days later from Heathrow to Pristina.

Following the Balkan conflicts in the late 1990s involving, amongst others, Serbian and Kosovan forces, the management of prisons in Kosovo was taken over by the UN Authority, in this case UNMIK. The prisons in Kosovo, particularly Dubrava Prison, near the Serbia/Kosovo border, had been the sites of terrible events and UNMIK were nervous of allowing the return of control of Kosovan prisons, and, more importantly, the prisoners in them, to the Kosovan Correctional Services (KCS). Emotions were still raw following the war. The prisons held many alleged war criminals and real hurt had been inflicted by the competing forces during the conflict. In particular, during the withdrawal of the Serbian Army through Kosovo back into Serbia, there had been much bloodshed at Dubrava Prison. The Serbians held the belief that Kosovo was, in fact, part of Serbia. The Kosovan Liberation army held a different view, and there had been much death and misery.

Too often, prisons are a distillation of all that is *wrong* with a particular society. In Kosovo, at that time, the perpetrators and the victims of conflict were concentrated within the walls of the same prisons. Those in UNMIK knew that there were real risks if the handover was not a success, and my findings would be key to when, or whether, that handover took place.

During my review, I was given unfettered access to all Kosovan correctional facilities. Dubrava Prison gave me an invaluable perspective on the problems of imprisonment in a not yet wholly stable society, where the tensions were just, only just, below the surface.

Dubrava Prison is the largest prison in Kosovo. It has had a troubled past. The ethnic trouble and warfare during the 1990s have left their mark. When I visited, Serbian prisoners were not held in Dubrava, and there were no Serbian members of staff. When I arrived, I met the two directors of the prison. In recognition of the plan to hand control of prisons from the UN to the Kosovan Correctional Service (KCS), there was an international director and a KCS director. During one of our early conversations, both of them told me that they had concerns about the security of the prison and were very keen to hear my views once I had spent some time there.

The prison had experienced a number of major incidents, including the breakout of 14 Category A prisoners who had overpowered staff, using tools that had been stored on the wing, and smashed their way through the wire fences. They had reached the perimeter wall, where they were met by armed accomplices on the other side. A firefight ensued between the accomplices and the Romanian special police unit, part of UNMIK, which was guarding the perimeter. Realising that the escape had been compromised, the 14 Category A prisoners had returned to their block.

As a former governor of a high-security prison, I found this horrifying, and I understood the nervousness of the authorities and the high stakes involved in operating prisons and trying to manage a return to stability and control. This then was the background against which I visited Dubrava Prison over two days.

The prison was in a fairly isolated part of North West Kosovo. There was a large apron of land around the prison and access was via a long road, protected by two manned vehicle checkpoints before the wall was reached.

The prison wall was five metres high and was topped with razor wire. The wall bore testimony to the war, with large shell holes at points along the perimeter wall. Dubrava's accommodation comprised eight living units, seven with wire mesh fence individually around them. Block 1, which held the Category A prisoners, had a double-skinned wire fence around it with razor wire on top of it and a sterile area.

Access to the accommodation unit for Block 1, where the Category A prisoners were held, was via electronic, interlocking gates, which were controlled from a discrete security area, colloquially known as the 'bubble.' One of the major failures in the system during the failed escape attempt was that prisoners were able to gain access to the bubble from within the accommodation unit and therefore gain access to the control of the electronic gates. There was limited use of CCTV cameras around Block 1, with four cameras being used, although on the first day of my visit one of these cameras was inoperative.

When I looked at the security procedures in place at Dubrava, I had real and serious concerns. In just one visit over two days I identified a number of concerns and saw practices that I viewed as totally unacceptable for a prison holding dangerous prisoners who had demonstrated their appetite for escape and violence. What I saw led me to conclude that staff were neither interacting appropriately with nor were in proper control of prisoners. These were just some of the security failures I saw during the two days I was in Dubrava:

- Visitors to the prison being asked to remove coats and bags before walking through a metal detector portal. The coats and bags were then passed to them around the side of the portal and weren't searched.

- Many cells with their observation panels blocked by prisoners so that staff had no view into them. When I asked for one of these cells to be unlocked, so that I could speak to the prisoners, I found five prisoners locked into a four-man cell, to the embarrassment of staff. When I questioned the misplaced prisoner, he said he just wanted to be with his mates.

- Throughout the establishment, staff were carrying keys in their hands or their pockets, without them being attached to a key chain. I later spotted a large box full of key chains sitting unused under a desk in an office.

- Category A prisoners on the exercise yard who had taken off the orange tabards they were supposed to wear. It was only when I pointed this out to the staff supervising the exercise yard that the prisoners were asked to put on their identifying clothing.

As I walked around the prison, I saw large groups of staff who seemed to be doing very little. On one unit, I counted 22 correctional officers just standing around chatting to one another, whilst all the prisoners were locked in their cells. The international director of the prison had told me about the regime that she had introduced to improve access to activities for prisoners, but I saw very little evidence of any such regime actually happening. On paper, Dubrava had the highest levels of prisoner employment of any Kosovan prison, but that amounted only to one prisoner in ten and, clearly, that was not routinely achieved.

The interactions I saw between staff and prisoners on the accommodation units suggested to me that staff were unsure and uneasy, despite there being plenty of them. When I saw prisoners exercising, in secured compounds, there was hardly any interaction between them and the staff supervising. Staff seemed to coalesce in groups with other staff, probably because they felt safer in numbers, and I had real concerns about the ability of staff to maintain professional relationships with prisoners. Many members of staff of various grades told me that they found it difficult to remain professionally detached, especially when they were dealing with those who were alleged to have committed war crimes and those suspected of involvement in serious organised crime.

Given the obvious strength of feelings amongst staff and prisoners, and the continuing impact of the conflict on all who had suffered it, I knew that decency, the way all prisoners were treated by staff, could prove a real challenge at Dubrava. In fact, I saw many examples of staff who were enthusiastic and focussed on the work they did and no evidence of any mistreatment of prisoners. The food was good; I tasted it myself and prisoners told me they had few complaints about it too. The accommodation, though spartan and cramped by UK standards, was clean and, just as at home, prisoners worked as cleaners and orderlies to keep communal areas clean and tidy.

I was keen to see the segregation unit and was pleasantly surprised, when I did, that it held only five prisoners. The cells in the unit were of an acceptable standard, but I was concerned to be told that all bedding and mattresses were removed from the cells during the day so that the prisoners could not sleep or lie down comfortably. This felt unnecessary and less than decent. I did see one prisoner lying on the bare, sheet metal base of his bed, trying to sleep, and he told me he had not yet been found guilty of any offence against prison rules. Nobody, from the officer in the segregation unit to the director, could enlighten me as to on what authority a prisoner awaiting adjudication could be kept in those conditions.

At the end of my two days, I fed back to the two directors and I later incorporated my assessment of Dubrava into my report, which would inform the decision on the transfer of powers. The only conclusion I could draw, from what I had seen and what I had been told, was that Dubrava was a prison where staff were not properly in control and where there was an absence of management 'grip' at the lower levels.

I met the five international staff provided by the UN to support local managers and provide mentoring to the KCS staff. These were professionally brave and committed individuals and they were keen to work with staff across the prison, but they had been given offices in an administration block outside the prison, which made this almost impossible.

Sadly, within three months of my visit and report, a group of Category A prisoners escaped from Dubrava. It had, really, only ever been a matter of 'when', not 'if'.

21

High-Security Prisons

As I approached the end of my career in the Prison Service, I was appointed as the director of high security, and a member of the National Offender Management Services (NOMS) Board.

I would be lying if I said I did not feel the weight of responsibility in that role. It is a gaoler's pride (forgive me) that, during my tenure as director of high security, no Category A prisoner escaped from custody. I was in no doubt, as director, that this was the single most important indicator that the high-security estate was doing its job. To place that in perspective, I should look at how the high-security arrangements in UK prisons had evolved.

For almost a century before the mid-1960s, prisons in England and Wales had not changed in any meaningful way. If you were sent to prison, you were taken from the court, through a large gate, behind a big wall and kept there until the sentence of the court had been carried out. This occurred whether you were serving seven days for non-payment of a fine or a life sentence for murder; there was no difference.

Then, in the 1960s, a series of events occurred that seriously shook public faith in the Prison Service, and which showed that the Prison Service was not fit for purpose. In July

1965 the Great Train Robber, Ronnie Biggs, was sprung from Wandsworth after only 15 months inside; he scaled the wall with a rope ladder and dropped onto the roof of a removal van that was waiting on the other side of the wall. Eleven months earlier, another member of the gang, Charlie Wilson, had escaped from Winson Green prison in Birmingham, four months into a 30-year sentence.

Of even greater embarrassment to the Prison Service and to the British government was the fact that in 1966 the Russian spy, George Blake, who was serving a sentence of 42 years, escaped from Wormwood Scrubs and has remained unlawfully at large ever since.

These events shook the Prison Service to its foundation and the Home Office, then responsible for it, decided that something had to be done. 'Something must be done' is usually a Civil Service euphemism for 'we must have an inquiry or an investigation'. In this case the matter was so serious that, to give credibility to the process, a significant public figure was appointed to lead the investigation and to make recommendations. Lord Louis Mountbatten was selected for the role. Years later, Mountbatten was murdered by criminals whom his recommendations would have placed in the high-security category his inquiry recommended.

The Mountbatten Inquiry was far reaching and excellent. It produced some significant benefits to the Prison Service that have stood the test of time and which still pertain in 2017.

The inquiry created the rank of senior officer as a supervisor of front-line prison officers; it introduced the use of UHF radios to improve communications, the use of dogs to improve security and, crucially, the concept of categorisation. This concept was central to the way the modern Prison Service operates in the UK. From then on, prisoners were not seen as a homogeneous group, regardless of their offence, sentence length or the risk they presented. Under the post-Mountbatten categorisation system, each prisoner was differentiated and categorised based upon his dangerousness to the public.

There are now four categories of prisoner: A, B, C and D, with D being applied to those prisoners considered to present the least risk and Category A reserved for those prisoners who are '... so dangerous to the police, the state or the public, that escape must be made impossible'. Having recommended this categorisation system, Mountbatten went on to recommend that Category A prisoners should be concentrated in an 'escape-proof prison', probably on the Isle of Wight. Mountbatten believed that 19th-century prison buildings, particularly where there was also overcrowding, made some escapes inevitable and that, at the time of his inquiry, the Prison Service did not have any prisons that could be considered to be really secure.

The Home Office was appreciative of the significant improvements that Mountbatten proposed, but uneasy about the recommendation that the most dangerous prisoners should be concentrated in one place. There were various objections to the idea of a single maximum-security prison. Officials were nervous that, were something to go seriously wrong in a prison holding all of the most dangerous prisoners in the country, it would be nothing short of a 'nuclear event'. The mandarins in Whitehall also felt that it would not be possible to have a humane regime that was predicated upon security alone.

And so, the official mind did what the official mind does when it doesn't like a recommendation of an inquiry; it had another inquiry. This second inquiry was headed by Professor Leon Radzinowicz from the Cambridge Institute of Criminology, a significant figure in the criminology world. Radzinowicz looked at the same facts as Mountbatten and, unsurprisingly, came up with a completely different solution to the question of where to hold prisoners in the highest security category.

Radzinowicz said that, rather than concentrating the most dangerous prisoners, the Category A prisoners, in one place, they should be dispersed; that is, they should be in a diluted population of high-end Category B prisoners, those prisoners who don't quite make the threshold to be considered Category A, but cannot be trusted in lesser security conditions. Radzinowicz recommended that the Category A prisoners and high-end Category B prisoners should be dispersed to a number of high-security prisons. This recommendation was much more to the liking of the Home Office mandarins and was accepted and, thus, the dispersal system was born.

With one or two notable glitches, the dispersal system has served the Prison Service well for over 50 years.

When I became director of high security, I took responsibility for the eight high-security prisons: Frankland, near Durham; Full Sutton, near York; Wakefield; Manchester; Long Lartin, in Worcestershire; Woodhill, in Milton Keynes; Whitemoor, in Cambridgeshire and Belmarsh, in London.

All Category A prisoners were held in one of these eight prisons. The number of Category A prisoners in the system was remarkably steady, with just under 1,000 prisoners being designated Category A at any time. These 1,000 or so Category A prisoners were diluted or dispersed with about 5,000 high-end Category B prisoners, making a total population in the high-security estate of 6,000 souls.

High-security prisons are very complex and have, historically, been very difficult places to work in and to live in. However, in my view, and I feel confident in saying this, the system works, since it protects the public by securely, and humanely, containing the 'heavy end' prisoners within the system. This is important as many of the prisoners held in the high-security prisons will, effectively, be housed there for much, if not all, of their lives. So, it is important that they have something to hold onto, because, without hope, there is only despair and with despair comes violence, either against themselves or others.

These prisons also hold those special units necessary to hold prisoners who cannot safely be held in the mainstream high-security population. The only protected witness unit in the prison system is in the high-security estate. The close supervision centres, which accommodate the most violent of men, who have demonstrated that they are willing to deploy severe violence, including murder, in prison, are located within the high-security estate. There were close supervision centres in Whitemoor, Woodhill and Wakefield prisons. While men in the close supervision centres are kept under constant review, it is fair to say that some in the system may never leave that severely restricted system, due to their dangerousness. Similarly, there are units at Frankland and Whitemoor prisons that are set up to deal with dangerous and severely personality-disordered prisoners. This is extremely taxing and demanding work and only carried out within the high-security prisons.

In addition to these units, all high-security prisons have a number of prisoners who are being dealt with under the 'Managing Challenging Behaviour' scheme.

So, high-security prisons work, they operate predicated upon the primacy of security, and security is absolutely essential, but is not sufficient to discharge our duty to those in our custody. Our primary duty is to make escape impossible, as required explicitly in the definition of a Category A prisoner, but we must also ensure that we deal humanely with men whom many of the public might consider do not merit this consideration. This can be a challenge, but for all of those working in prisons it is crucial that our own standards prevail.

Almost every prisoner who is well known to the public is held in a high-security prison and there are frequent bouts of moral outrage in the 'red tops' about some event or other regarding so-called 'monsters'. But the significant 'keep you awake at night' concern for governors of high-security prisons is escape.

Just to place it in context, the last time anybody escaped from a high-security prison, the governor was sacked; the area manager was sacked; the director general of the Prison Service was sacked; the prisons' minister was sacked and the home secretary hung on by his fingernails: it is serious stuff.

22

Locked into the Legend

I ended my Prison Service career as director of high security. Over the course of my long career in the high-security arm of the estate, I regularly met the same prisoners and came to know them quite well.

A number of these men had come to believe in their so-called prison legends. These were, usually, 'hard men', by which I mean they did not shy away from confrontation and violence. They acted like gunslingers, and had reputations to keep up.

As these men got older, a new generation of younger, harder men walked the landings, ready to go head to head with these old-time legends. The result wouldn't have been pretty. It therefore suited the ageing 'legends' to huff and puff while hiding safely in segregation units or close supervision centres, where they could cling on to their reputation without the need to actually defend it.

Mr A:

'YOU FUCKING CAN'T!' he shouted in my face.

I wondered what I was forbidden to do. He was obviously very angry; his face was red and contorted as he spat the words out. I said, 'What can't I do?'

He just repeated, 'You fucking can't'.

Eventually, I worked out that what he was saying was being distorted by his faux cockney accent and that, rather than forbidding me from doing something, he was drawing an unflattering comparison between me and the female anatomy. To the uninitiated, he must have sounded as though he'd been born inside one of the Bow bells. As it happens, he was born, and raised, in the home counties. Apparently, being a London gangster carries more 'cred' than being a prisoner from these more affluent parts.

The first time I'd met Mr A was in Bristol Prison in the 1980s, when he was on what was euphemistically called a 'lie down' from Long Lartin Prison. That is, he had been transferred, due to his bad behaviour, for 28 days, to give the Long Lartin staff some respite. In the special cell, which is a bare concrete box, he was completely naked, having refused to wear the canvas clothing provided. As duty governor, I went in to speak to him. He was loud, aggressively threatening, and had cleverly written 'I want a brain scan' in his excrement on the wall.

I saw him, off and on, throughout my career and our interactions didn't improve in quality over the years. On one unhappy occasion when I was duty governor at Whitemoor, I was carrying out governor's adjudications. He was brought in front of me, having been charged with yet another offence against prison rules. I was looking down, recording the officer's version of events in writing, when I heard a kerfuffle and looked up to see that a noble and self-sacrificing senior officer had thrown himself across the table between Mr A and me, to prevent the spit that Mr A had ejected in my direction from hitting me. This was something of a repeated pattern and, much later, on another occasion at Wakefield prison, he did indeed succeed in spitting in my face. This time, getting older worked in my favour since I was now wearing glasses.

Every time I saw him I received a deluge of abuse. He truly was a lost soul. He would never last long on the landings due to his self-aggrandising attitude, and was, therefore locked in, hiding in near seclusion while pretending not to be. The sad thing was, he probably thought that was a result, an achievement, proof of his ability to 'beat the system'.

Mr B: was a 'hard man'; he had fought for the British heavyweight boxing title, spoke with a strong Yorkshire accent and clearly had his own set of rules where right was right, and wrong was everyone else. He was frequently restrained by staff and gave a good account of himself, although was always eventually subdued. I quite liked him.

I did not think of him for many years until a documentary was being made at one of the high-security prisons for which I was now responsible. I became aware that his son was serving a life sentence in that prison. I spoke with the son, who was not of the same cut as his father. I was, however, further surprised when, on a later visit to another high-security prison, Long Lartin, I heard his name. I presumed it must be him; I went to see him. I didn't recognise the man before me, although he looked a bit like him. I said, 'Who are you?' and it quickly became clear that I was talking to another son of this man, who was also serving a life sentence. It would seem to be the family business. I asked him about his father and he said he had died in a drink-related incident. 'What was the incident?' I asked.

'Just drink'.

At least he died outside of prison.

Mr C: wasn't much to look at but he was decisive in his actions. The first time I became aware of him was when he was on remand and, on being produced at court, he attempted to escape by throwing himself through a large glass window on the second floor. This was impressive, although I do not believe that the officer he was handcuffed to, and who was taken on the journey through the window with him, was impressed.

His offence was almost an adventure involving kidnap, ransom demands, and much being chased across the country, but it was an adventure with severe costs to innocent individuals, and he was a strange mix of intelligent and incredibly stupid. He spoke well, using long words, sometimes in the right context, and he affected cultural aspirations but he was, at bottom, a bit of a prat, but a dangerous prat, who successfully escaped from a high-security prison with two others (before my time as director of high security) and was at large for some days, eventually being recaptured a dozen miles from the prison.

This brought him into the special secure units, which are, effectively, very secure prisons inside very secure prisons.

I hadn't seen him for many years. I didn't even know that he had clocked me. But after many years, as I walked into the special secure unit at Whitemoor prison, someone started playing 'Danny Boy' on a small organ. It was an electronic organ and, standing behind it, looking at me and playing this tune, was Mr C, with a decidedly pleased expression on his face. 'Hello, how are you?' I said to him.

'Never better,' he said with a smile, to which I thought, 'Well, you must have very low expectations.'

I learned a valuable lesson here, which was that, if you are serving a very long prison sentence, and are of a particular mindset, you will have every single minute, of every hour, of every day, of every year to think of nothing but your sense of grievance and your desired outcomes. Those of us who are not prisoners only hire out for 40 hours a week or so; it is not really fair. Whereas most of us work 40 hours per week for pay, people like Mr C work 168 hours per week for payback.

Mr D: was a lost soul. Unlike others, he didn't seek to project himself as a legend but, rather, behaved in such a bizarre manner that he had to be treated differently to others. His original offence was unremarkable, involving theft and burglary, but it was exacerbated by his attempt to get his cellmate to hang himself in prison. He manipulated and bullied him and almost succeeded in persuading him to kill himself. He found himself in the high-security estate, then in the close supervision centre and he yo-yoed between various parts of this and special hospitals. Nobody was sure if he was bad or mad, but it didn't really matter; he was a dangerous man, mostly to himself.

He was the only man I ever met who appeared completely impervious to pain. When prison officers had to use control and restraint techniques on him, and other prisoners would have been screaming for the pain to stop, he just carried on. His MO was to self-harm and his actions became increasingly bizarre. He would insert objects into his body at various points that would make you screw up your eyes and cross your legs thinking about it. It was a certainty that one day he would die at his own hands. He would die from septicaemia or otherwise succeed in seriously harming himself, internally.

Mostly it was a case of attention seeking, but it was a high-risk business. I had tried, at various times in my career, to gain some sort of agreement with him to find a way forward and I think that he tried his best, but he could not sustain the required behaviour for the required length of time.

I learned, some years after I last saw him, that he had died of blood poisoning.

Mr E: was the only survivor of a notorious terrorist atrocity, which he, and others, perpetrated. He didn't speak English very well. He was socially isolated within the prison, as other prisoners didn't like his 'blowing up people' crime. Most of them just couldn't see the profit in it. Despite frequent contact with him, I never gained the impression that he was either religiously or politically driven. He always seemed somewhat detached and very aware of (what he thought was) his importance. He became lost in the system and spent long periods of time in the segregation units of high-security prisons.

I would speak with him frequently as part of my governor's rounds. He always wanted something and, if he needed it and was entitled to it, he got it; if he merely wanted it, he did not. I spent much of my time saying 'no' to him. I saw him almost daily, as I walked around the prison, and he always had a want, or sometimes a need. Typically, he would say, 'I need to phone my legal rep', and I'd say, 'I'll arrange for that to happen.' Conversely, when he said things like, 'I want a TV in my cell', I'd say, 'Until your behaviour improves, you won't get access to a TV'. I did, though, always ensure that he had something to read. He was not grateful.

One day, when staff opened his cell door in the segregation unit so that I could speak to him, he looked me straight in the eye and said, 'This is personal now; I know where you live, I know what car you drive, I know what car your wife drives, I know where your children go to school. This is serious; I know everything about you, Governor McDonald'.

A threatened man lives long, I thought, or at least I hoped. I think he is still in prison. And my name's still McAllister.

Mr F: didn't kill people. He got people to kill people. He had a merciless, manipulative mind. He was always one step removed whenever 'it', whatever 'it' was, happened. Eventually he found himself in the most secure part of the most secure prison, in the most secure part of the prison system, where he spent his time legally challenging everything that was done to him.

I don't mind this; if they are writing, they are not fighting. But, to give you an indication of his mentality, I visited him once and saw that he had put in a complaint, saying that it was his 'human right to have more gravy with his dinner'.

Mr G: was a hit man. He had come to this country from far away and taken a number of mundane jobs. He had then discovered that violence paid more than working, so he forged a career carrying out hits. These were purely financial transactions; no sentiment involved. His clients got what they paid for and he got money. He had been duly convicted and brought into the high-security system.

I always found him to be cheerful and hardworking, ready with a smile. However, as a gun for hire he would attack anyone for two ounces of tobacco, without compunction. This became apparent when he beat another prisoner senseless, though he didn't even know him. Word had it that, if you wanted more than a beating, it cost a bit more, though not much more.

When I last saw him, he was still in a high-security prison. I visited Frankland as director of high security and became aware that Mr G was in the segregation unit there. When staff opened his cell door, his face lit up and he greeted me like a long-lost friend: 'Hello Mr McAllister, good to see you. You're looking well'. He looked exactly the same as he had done years ago when he came to Whitemoor, when I had been the governor.

He was an extreme example of someone who was totally amoral, but even he had a softer side, when he talked about the family he had left behind: a family he would never see again. He could have spent what little money he earned in prison on himself, as most prisoners do. When he wasn't being held in the segregation unit, he could work in one of the jobs available: typically humdrum, repetitive packing jobs. What little he earned, he sent back to his family in his own country. To a family he would never see again, in a land he would never see again.

When I last saw him, despite his advancing age, he looked strong and fit and was still smiling. He was being held in yet another segregation unit for carrying out yet another hit, seriously injuring another prisoner, this time using a blade. He told me that he had no bad feeling towards his victim; it was just business.

Recently, he made the papers for murdering another prisoner.

Mr H: was built like a brick wall. A former bouncer, he was a bag of uncontrolled aggression and had murdered a man. While on remand, he had written to the female governor of the prison in which he was being held, offering her enormous amounts of cocaine in return for various personal services for him. She demurred. He came to Bristol on a 'lie down', a short transfer to give staff at his own prison a rest from him, some respite from his violence, and proved a real handful for Bristol staff. Eventually he was convicted and sent into a dispersal prison.

The level of his violence knew no bounds and he finally carried out a very serious assault on a prison officer; truly horrendous. The prison officer never worked again. He went into the close supervision system, where he remains many, many years later and it is difficult to see him not being there for ever and ever, Amen.

When I first met **Mr J**, he was on remand for a notorious, sexually motivated murder of a young boy. He was another built like a brick wall, who exuded aggression, towards others and towards himself; he was an extremely angry man.

On the day he tried to assault me, staff moved quickly to contain him. He had made a request at governor's applications, which I was hearing, I had denied the request and he tried to get me to change my mind by lunging at me across the desk. Staff, alert to the risk, were ready for him and he didn't get near me, to his great annoyance.

I did not see him again for 20 years. When I did finally see him, in Full Sutton Prison, I couldn't believe it was the same man. He had shrunk to half his size. Where the scowl had been, there was now an ingratiating smile. He was timid – not because anything had happened to him, nobody had done anything to him – he'd just grown old.

It is hard to be intimidating when you rely on a Zimmer. Although, probably some of them will continue to try. It's sad really, but what can they do, they have their reputations to think of.

23

Do-Gooders

Nothing attracts self-appointed experts as routinely and with as much passion as the Prison Service does. Sometimes this involves the 'Mr Toad', that self-appointed expert, variety, sometimes their motivation is a relative housed within the system who needs protection. A few are odd and deluded, while others style themselves as professional experts and pop up whenever a quote or comment on prisons is needed.

The 'Mr Toad' do-gooder has generally had a brush with the system him or herself, often an oblique, fleeting look into the 'belly of the beast'. Sometimes there has been no physical contact with the system, rather a vicarious interest, but the effect is just the same. 'Mr Toad' believes that not only can he see the flaws in the system to which everyone else is apparently blind, but he can see the remedies, as plain as the nose on your face. 'Mr Toad' brings nothing to the penal debate but his misinformed opinions. He lacks knowledge and is burdened by self-belief; the system is his hobby. He would be an irrelevance but for the fact that the official mind cannot receive a letter, e-mail or telephone call without setting up a correspondence file. Every query must be responded to, on target and, often, copied widely, drawing other officials into the web. The persistent 'Mr Toad' , once he has learned this, can amuse himself for months, years. He can have a whole array of officials answering his pedantic, unfocused and often plain irrelevant concerns. 'Mr Toad's queries clog up the system again and again.

I have always believed that every legitimate concern should be addressed to ensure that those within the system are not disadvantaged. When that has been done, and done to the best of the official ability, I have found that the only effective response when 'Mr Toad' responds yet again is to send the 'I have nothing that I can usefully add to my letter of...' letter; and keep sending it as required.

The concerned relative or friend has a more solid reason for addressing the system. These are the people driven by the desire to help someone they care about who is within the system. I can only applaud this, though an over-confrontational and challenging approach often sees the establishment pull up the drawbridge, or even respond in an equally confrontational manner. The calm, reasonable and persistent approach is, usually, reciprocated. It is a re-affirming experience to come across a mum, dad, aunt or brother who is seeking to look after their own. Were I on the other side of the system, I would want someone sticking up for me.

There are of course people who are not relatives of those in prison but who seek to champion individual cases. These range from the truly altruistic individuals who believe a miscarriage of justice has taken place, to those who simply believe in the benefits of prison visits.

One organisation that works within, but not as part of, the system, is the National Association of Prison Visitors (NAPV). Under the NAPV umbrella, ordinary members of the public visit prisoners to offer friendship and 'share normality'. I have never analysed what it is, exactly, that motivates individuals to undertake prison visits but I'm glad it happens.

Victim awareness courses and restorative justice projects attempt to reconcile the worlds of perpetrators of crimes and the victims of those crimes. They are usually run by volunteers from outside the prison, often, but not always, linked to religious and church groups. In my time, I had a rather cynical view of these worthy initiatives and of prisoners' reasons for engaging with them. I know that, if I were in prison and I could ameliorate my conditions or shorten my sentence by paying lip service to being sorry and recognising the harm I had done, then I would say whatever I had to say; most of us would. So, for a long time, I viewed these approaches as well-meaning but open to exploitation by some prisoners.

I changed my mind, though, when, at Whitemoor Prison, I saw what I genuinely believe were real changes in attitude on the part of some prisoners. These were young men I had come to know as cynical manipulators who thought only of themselves. A group of volunteers, part of an organisation called 'Prison Fellowship', had come into the prison to run a course called 'The Sycamore Tree', which put victims of crime and prisoners together. Despite my early doubts, I saw real change in some men when they got a glimpse of the impact of crimes such as those they had committed on victims. The 'victim' was revealed to be an ordinary person who had suffered, through no fault of theirs, as a consequence of a crime. I wouldn't want to overstate it, these were no Damascene conversions, but for some men the concept of empathy was born. That was a good thing.

Independent Monitoring Boards (IMBs), formerly known as Boards of Visitors, are groups of people who form a committee in every prison establishment. Appointed by the Justice Minister, they are the eyes and ears of the public, or the Minister, if you like, within the prison. There is, often, a lack of clarity as to their role. Some governors' view is that they act on behalf of individual prisoners only. However, IMB members have the right to access not only any prisoner but also any, and all, parts of a prison at any time. This can only be a good thing, and an important check on the, often hidden, work going on behind prison walls. In the best situations the IMB works constructively within the system to the benefit of prisoners, staff and the greater good. In the worst situations, however, the IMB attempts to assert a quasi-managerial role, which inevitably leads to conflict with the prison management. It is for individual governors to decide on a modus operandi with the IMB in their prison, so that members can work constructively in their intended role, whilst not allowing them to stray into executive areas.

A major flaw in the IMB system is that the boards are, on the whole, representative of those people who send offenders to prison, but not representative of the people sent to prison. They are not representative of the whole of society. They are, generally, white, middle-class, middle-aged and middle-minded, and there are not too many white, middle-class, middle-aged and middle-minded prisoners. There are some exceptions to the above but boards continuously fail to attract a more representative cross section of society to join them. Having said that, the individual members of the IMBs bring the benefits of a voluntary ethos, experience of life and commitment to decency, a realistic view of what is right, what is possible and what is appropriate in all the circumstances. Prisons are better places for the presence of IMBs; they shine a light into the system.

The Prisons Inspectorate (HMIP), is another statutory body that reviews the performance of prisons. HMIP provides a necessary check and balance but suffers from serious flaws. The first of these is that it is very easy to come into a prison and say what should be done, while wholly ignoring the resource implications. I have repeatedly seen governors told by HMIP, 'you should do this'. When the governor states there is no funding to do 'this', the HMIP response is often 'that's not our problem'.

HMIP seems to operate in a world of black and white, when in reality the world has many shades of grey. When HMIP labelled HMYOI Brinsford a 'stain on the Prison Service', and nine months later labelled it 'an establishment transformed', I was personally grateful, but also uneasy. I knew how much work had been done in a year but I also knew that the establishment had not been black then, and was not white now. It had been a matt mucky grey then, and was a shiny pearly grey a year later. In truth, the HMIP reports do, to some extent, show the gradations, but it is in the foreword to each published report that the damage is done. The press, in particular, often look no further than the juicy soundbite left prominently for them in the introduction.

'Well-run prison has quiet day' is not a common *Sun* headline.

Often, in my view, people who cannot, or are unwilling to, do the job yet are perfectly willing to tell those doing the job where they are going wrong have a serious credibility issue. Running a prison is a difficult and demanding job. Working in a prison is difficult and demanding. When staff have fought the good fight and struggled through the day, anyone who joins the battlefield at day end and bayonets the wounded is of no real assistance. In short there is a need for an inspectorate, but it must be founded in competence, credibility and reality.

Pressure groups such as NACRO (formerly The National Association for the Care and Resettlement of Offenders) and The Prison Reform Trust (PRT) are relevant and important organisations. I'm glad these exist too, though what they say can be uncomfortable.

Indeed, there is no shortage of people and organisations that keep the system honest. Despite the flaws and failings, they are a force for good. The Prison Service is made up of individuals with human flaws and failings. The Prison Service is also made up of generally decent, generally hardworking, generally well-intended, generally committed people trying to do a very complex and often difficult job with honesty and decency. We should welcome scrutiny, we should accommodate scrutiny and we should look fully to our beliefs, while making room for the doubts of others.

24

Libyan Prisons
Post-Revolution

Shortly after my retirement, I received a letter from the then director of the International Centre for Prison Studies (ICPS), asking me whether I would do some work with them in Libya, as the country tried to rebuild its institutions following the 2011 revolution and the overthrow of Colonel Gaddafi. The director told me that the prisons in Libya were in a state of flux, and the post-revolution government, the National Transitional Council (NTC), urgently needed support and advice if Libyan prisons were to operate securely, safely and with humanity.

I knew of the ICPS, a charity and research body that worked on a consultancy basis for international organisations, governmental and non-governmental. I thought it would be interesting to visit and report on Libyan prisons, and indeed it was. During my visits to Libya, I met many men and women who were working tirelessly to return their country to some normality, but I also saw evidence of the continuing factional violence that would, sadly, lead to another civil war in 2014.

Prisons in Libya are under the control of the judicial police, but after 2011 this was complicated by large numbers of revolutionary fighters who were very reluctant to cede control of prisons back to the judicial police when the end of the war was declared by the NTC. The judicial police appeared to have a thankless task; they were under-resourced and subject to capricious political interference at every turn. Prison governors were appointed, and removed, frequently, seemingly at the whim of politicians. That many judicial police officers, of all ranks, strived to provide safe, humane and secure prisons in a seemingly shambolic political landscape was greatly to their credit. Most of those I met were dedicated and resolute and treated me with great courtesy when I visited their prisons.

TRIPOLI LOCAL PRISON had, originally, functioned for low-risk, short-term prisoners from the lower courts. Since the revolution, it had received prisoners of all categories and, given that there was no meaningful classification system at the prison, the weight of the prisoners' alleged offences varied significantly. Pre-revolution the prison had held about 400 low-risk prisoners.

In April 2012 the prison population was 360 but by the time I visited in July 2012 it had risen to 560, most of whom were awaiting trial. It was clear, after even only a short time in the prison, that it was at a critical point and needed immediate action from the senior managers in the judicial police. A combination of serious overcrowding, the predictable continuing increase in the prisoner population, a lack of effective security and prisoner classification, poor prison management and the continuing lack of clarity about the conditions of service of the members of staff were, in my view and that of my ICPS colleagues, 'a recipe for disaster'.

On 10th August 2012 there was rioting and armed attacks on the prison, which resulted in the local prison becoming unusable and significant harm to individuals. I paid a further visit to Tripoli Local just after these events and heard various accounts of what had happened. What had happened was not altogether surprising, given our assessment, back in July, that 'the exercise yard is not in a very secure part of the prison'. With prisoners on the yard, armed groups attacked the area from outside. Although the fog of war had, by then, descended and there was a lack of clarity with regard to who was shooting at whom, at the end of the incident two prisoners were dead and four staff were injured. As well as these fatalities, 52 prisoners had escaped and most of them were still unlawfully at large. The prison was uninhabitable. All prisoners had to be decanted, most of them transferring to AL JAIBS PRISON, which I visited shortly after the final visit to Tripoli Local.

When I visited Al Jaibs, I was reassured to meet the new governor, Colonel A, whom I had met when he had participated in a security workshop earlier in the ICPS programme. Since that time, in addition to being appointed the governor of Al Jaibs, Colonel A had been given overall responsibility for security in the judicial police. He was, therefore, a significant player in the future of Libyan prisons and I had confidence in his abilities.

Al Jaibs prison was, I presumed, a replacement for the places that had been lost at Tripoli Local but, for some reason, the prison did not figure on any of the prison maps I had been given. All became clear when I spoke to Colonel A and learned that what was now Al Jaibs prison had, actually, been a facility used by the Ministry of the Interior to train intelligence agents, and which had been readily available following the necessary decant of Tripoli Local. The roll, when I visited, was 300, and the remaining decanted prisoners (there had been a roll of 526 on the day of the Local Prison disturbances) had been dispersed to prisons at Ain Zara and Tajoora Main as well as a facility at Tripoli Airport.

It soon became clear that the Al Jaibs facility was being used for containment rather than any constructive activity, a fact confirmed by Colonel A and others. There was a clear reluctance to show me around the facility and when I asked, I was told, 'There's nothing to see'. While I pressed gently on this, I felt that now was not the right time to pursue it. It should be noted that the atmosphere in the complex and amongst staff was fairly relaxed. I had ascertained that the present use of Al Jaibs was seen as temporary, although it was not clear what temporary meant, and that the medium to long-term provision of a local facility would be either at a refurbished Al Jadeda prison or by the provision of a new-build prison.

One of the main reasons for this visit to Al Jaibs was to enlist the support of Colonel A for the ICPS work and I was delighted that his response to my visit, and the proposed ICPS work, was positive. However, the truly surprising event was that in the course of the visit to Al Jaibs, whereas previously ICPS had been unable to gain access to main players in the judicial police I was suddenly faced with a surfeit of access. The director general, Colonel B, made himself available and was positive and constructive, pledging his support for the Libya Project. Surprisingly, Mr C, who had been notable by his absence and his reluctance to engage with ICPS, suddenly appeared and again was very positive and friendly. Furthermore, Colonel D, who was the new Head of Training, made himself available to ICPS and once again was positive.

It became clear that, if there had been a breakdown in communication with regards to the Libya Project between the ICPS and the judicial police, we were now forgiven. In addition to being supportive of the project, Colonel B, the director general, discussed in some detail his perceived concerns with regard to security and training for the judicial police working in Libyan prisons. This was constructive and positive, and boded well for the future. However, there was a worrying indication that the director general had formed a view that the disturbance at the Tripoli Local Prison was caused by staff being too concerned about prisoners' rights and not sufficiently focused on security. I noted this, as an indication of the need for the right balance between human rights concerns and the security agenda.

I had some concerns about the continuing use of Al Jaibs, where there appeared to be little, if any, regime activities and few aspirations for prisoners beyond simple containment. As to Tripoli Local Prison, it was clear that it had shortcomings with regard to physical and dynamic security, which eventually led to the serious disturbance, and that shortcomings in procedural security impacted upon how the disturbances were resolved. There were too many prisoners and their alleged and actual offences were too weighty for the type of security the prison could provide. Indeed, outside of the cellular cages there was no effective security other than armed perimeter staff. With regards to procedural security the major failure was due to a lack of any meaningful categorisation; not only at Tripoli Local but throughout prisons in Libya. This meant that it was difficult to distinguish between low-level prisoners with regards to offences and prisoners charged with much more weighty offences such as murder and war crimes.

Shortly after visiting Al Jaibs, I went to AL JADEDA WOMEN'S PRISON, accompanied by A, First Secretary from the British Embassy in Tripoli, and Major B of the judicial police Strategic Planning Team.

On the morning of my visit the unlock roll was 51. Of these, 25 were Libyan citizens, 16 were sub-Saharan African women and all of the others were non-Libyan Arab women. I was surprised to learn that, from this total of 51 unlocked, only two of the prisoners were sentenced. There were six babies in the prison; most of these were with their mothers, although in the governor's office I became aware of a baby sleeping on a bed in the corner. Captain C, the deputy governor, who was in charge on the day I visited, told me that this baby had been rejected by its mother, who suffered mental health issues and was HIV positive. Staff were taking it in turns to care for this baby until a more permanent solution could be brokered through social workers. As I walked around the prison, I saw another case where a baby could only be with his mother intermittently, as the mother's behaviour was so erratic.

This woman was being kept separate from other prisoners, although not in the segregation unit. She was in a dormitory by herself with her baby and staff explained to us that this young woman could be very aggressive and angry. There was a particular concern with regards to the mother being HIV positive and the baby not yet thriving, being extremely small for a two-month-old. It was clear that staff and doctors were doing all that they could to support this woman, who presented as cheerful when I first met her, although in the course of the visit she became aggressive and had to be locked up.

At the time I visited, Captain C herself was just about to go on maternity leave and I knew that her loss would be felt by everyone in the prison. She was an impressive operator and a significant player in the Justice Department's Strategic Planning Team. Over sweet tea in the governor's office, Captain C informed me that the prison was stable but that there was, currently, a difficulty with regards to procurement and she had had to buy some items for prisoners from her own pocket. Although she assured me that she had been reimbursed by the judicial police, this appeared to me to be indicative of a system that was not getting the simple things, so crucial in prison, right.

I went to the healthcare facility and staff there told me of the rota of doctors, dentists and other clinicians who visited the prison. The women's prison shared a clinic building with the male prisons at Al Jadeda, but I was concerned to hear that this had still not reopened following the disturbances that saw the male prisons at Al Jadeda severely damaged and taken out of action. In spite of this, the medical provision seemed adequate, other than an acute shortage of medication, which gave me real concerns. According to Captain C, the prison had about 20% of the medication it needed and any shortfall was made up via donations from non-governmental organisations and civil societies. This 'hand to mouth' system was far from ideal and, potentially, dangerous.

As I walked around the rest of the prison, I saw that the staffing situation, in general, was good, other than a shortage of about six social care workers, which, with Al Jadeda's population, was a significant shortfall. In all parts of the prison I visited the atmosphere was, generally, relaxed. Captain C told me that managers focused on providing a healthy environment, and acceptable food.

The regime was somewhat limited with two hours in the open air through the course of the day, one visit to the library a week and some limited gym facility available, although the gym equipment was somewhat damaged. Other than that, the women seemed to amuse themselves by communing with each other. The women tended to converge in self-selecting groups so that, for example, Libyan women would, generally, be in a dormitory with only Libyan women. The African women, similarly, tended to be self-selecting in their own community and the non-Libyan Arab women tended to keep to themselves. In spite of this, I neither saw nor heard of any evidence of animosity between the groupings.

There was an entitlement to a visit once a week. For Libyan nationals there was a requirement that the visitor was a blood relative but for non-Libyan nationals this was more relaxed. I saw a visit taking place between a mother and son in a visits room that was bare but clean. There was no barrier between the mother and son and the visit was carrying on in a relaxed manner, being supervised but not in an oppressive way.

Although for women at Al Jadeda there was a limited regime, I was encouraged to see that the programme for the regime was published and was known to prisoners. The relationship between staff and the women seemed sound. I was impressed by the caring leadership of Captain C and the caring attitude of her staff.

Overall I was impressed by the conditions in Al Jadeda Women's Prison. The atmosphere was not oppressive and, in most places, was relaxed. The availability of resources was optimised and staff were doing the best they could with what they had. On the very hot day that I visited, women could move in and out of the yard and there were chilled water coolers available in dormitories. The presenting difficulty was with regards to the lack of movement in the judicial system, and it is difficult to see how the cases for most of the women held in Al Jadeda could be progressed in the foreseeable future. Women who had not been convicted of any offence seemed destined to remain there until the system could process their cases more efficiently, and that still felt some way off.

A series of anti-tank obstacles peppered the road up to AINZARA prison. As I was driven up to the main gate, accompanied by Colonel A, Head of Judicial Police Training, I saw crowds of people; men, women and children, waiting to visit the prison. Many of them were carrying blankets and food to be passed to those they visited. It seemed strange to me that the men with machine guns guarding the perimeter were not wearing uniforms, but Colonel A explained that they were former revolutionaries who hadn't yet been issued with their new police uniforms. When we entered the perimeter of the prison it was noticeably cleaner than on my previous visits there and there was also less evidence of guns inside the prison. In the yard inside the perimeter there were, however, two heavy machine guns mounted on parked vehicles. I was greeted warmly by the deputy governor, Lieutenant Colonel C, who apologised that his boss, Sheikh B, had been called home due to a death in his family. Throughout this visit, and wherever we went, Lieutenant Colonel C, a career judicial police officer, was shadowed by an armed former revolutionary group member, now in judicial police uniform.

Part of Ainzara prison, known as Roemi prison, was, as it had been on my previous visits, off limits. This facility, which operated under the control of the Ministry of the Interior, was described to me as a 'political prison'. On the day I visited, the prison roll was 950, and once again most of the prisoners were pre-trial prisoners, with only a very small number of criminal cases having been heard and prisoners undergoing sentence. The prison was overcrowded; the roll had gone up by nearly 200 in the previous two months from 750, and this increase showed no signs of slowing down, as the criminal justice system was barely functioning and hardly any cases were being progressed through the courts.

Maintaining order and control was a challenge, as the prison held both former revolutionaries and those who had been loyal to Gaddafi. These two groups were effectively kept separate, although within the groupings, military and civil prisoners mixed freely. Such classification as was operating within the prison was predicated upon maintaining order and control, and not upon security.

The challenges facing the governor and his senior team included managing a staff group, many of whom were former revolutionaries now badged as judicial police officers. I had a long discussion with the deputy governor, in which he told me that he was very concerned about the shortage of staff and the training and deployment of those staff he had. Ainzara was, approximately, 120 staff short, with a current staffing level of 220. The ex-revolutionaries, now judicial police officers, were not yet operating as a uniform, disciplined group. The uniforms they wore were not, as they were meant to be, uniform, and some of the officers guarding the perimeter were still in civilian clothes. There were even some judicial police officers working inside the prison who were not in uniform, and who were, as a consequence, indistinguishable from prisoners. Given that the confusion with regards to who was shooting at whom was a major factor in the deaths and escapes from Tripoli Local Prison, this was a real concern and I advised Colonel C to get all of his accredited judicial police officers into a fully recognisable uniform as soon as he could. I was pleased to see, as we walked around the prison, still accompanied by the omnipresent revolutionary, that CCTV cameras had been fitted around the perimeter; I suggested that this would go some way towards reducing complete reliance on staff presence.

Ainzara had a new healthcare building, which was clean and modern but lacked any equipment. As expected, the equipment was 'on its way'. Similarly, with regards to medically qualified staff, the picture was not good: the two doctors working in the prison were, actually, medically qualified prisoners and so, other than for very minor first aid-type treatment, prisoners had to be taken to Al Jadeda prison hospital by ambulance.

From healthcare I went to the kitchen, where there were flies everywhere and the staff I saw were doing their best, in a kitchen that was too small and too dirty to manage more than the most basic meals for prisoners. That day, lunch was chicken and rice. I asked what would be served for the evening meal and learned that it would be... chicken and rice. Unsurprisingly, as I went around the prison speaking to prisoners, just as I would expect in any prison system, I witnessed prisoners complaining about the food on offer.

Visits provision at Ainzara was very much a 'work in progress' but a lot of thought had, clearly, gone into providing visits that were decent, but that did not compromise security unnecessarily. I saw an X-ray machine that was being used to screen visitors' property as it entered the establishment, with a clear indication, by signage, of what was, and was not, acceptable. Visits were being held in the open air, which, given the climate in Libya, seemed reasonable and imaginative. The visitors we saw in the establishment were being treated courteously and well.

Part of Ainzara was a facility known as 'The Italian prison'. This was, easily, the best accommodation in Ainzara. We were surprised, then, to see that this accommodation was being used only for pro-Gaddafi prisoners, many of whom were facing very serious charges of atrocities during the revolution. We were informed that access to the accommodation in the Italian prison was predicated upon good behaviour, and that all prisoners in this facility behaved to a high standard. It was unsurprising, therefore, to be made aware that, although there was a segregation unit, this was rarely used. All prisoners we spoke to in the Italian prison were open and friendly. Entrance to the cell blocks was through a large courtyard in which prisoners were sunning themselves in small numbers as I passed through. The cells themselves were not crowded, with, typically, two men in a cell that at one time would have held ten men. Cells had televisions and toilets and we formed a view that the prisoners in the Italian prison were very much from the 'officer class', and that their location, and the regime they enjoyed, reflected that.

If conditions in the Italian prison were acceptable, conditions in the major part of the prison, known as 'the tower block', were certainly not. An ongoing, somewhat chaotic refurbishment programme had led to large numbers of prisoners being held in abysmal conditions. We entered a cell about 40 feet long by 25 feet wide, in which more than 100 prisoners were being held. There was, literally, nowhere to walk, the whole area being covered by mattresses, and prisoners were just lying around. As soon as I entered this area I was, unsurprisingly, mobbed by prisoners, who complained to me about the poor conditions in which they were held. There were some toilets available, but they were few and far from clean.

I realised, as I walked around Ainzara, that, in addition to men who could clearly look after themselves, there were a number of individuals who were 'lost souls' in the system, including individuals with physical injuries and wounds and individuals with clear mental health needs. The overarching problem, as expressed by prisoners, was the lack of any movement whatsoever in the court system, and many men had been in prison for a very long time on relatively minor, alleged, offences, with no apparent light at the end of the tunnel. Other men, who were typically less clamorous, faced more serious charges and perhaps were in no hurry to approach the courts. Here, as in other Libyan prisons I visited, I couldn't get the refrain 'justice delayed is justice denied' out of my head.

In these terrible conditions, it was humbling that prisoners, in general, remained courteous and, indeed, although they had little, insisted on offering me their tea and biscuits. The human spirit prevails in even the most trying of conditions. The single television that we saw did not have an aerial, so one of the many crutches that were needed by the men in the unit was being used as a makeshift one. I was surprised, but pleasantly so, that none of the prisoners I met, or saw, were threatening or aggressive towards me, even when they were venting their individual and general complaints. I was also impressed by, and grateful for, the openness of the deputy governor at Ainzara, who allowed me to move amongst these prisoners, in these conditions, and see what was happening, warts and all.

It was abundantly clear that there were still tensions and anger between some ex-revolutionary guards and some prisoners. Some people told me that beatings and mistreatment were still happening and that some guards didn't understand or follow what the law allowed them to do. Of course, this was unacceptable and a concern, but I was reassured that any human rights abuses were not systemic and that the training to professionalise prison staff was a high priority for the Justice Ministry.

When I visited, there was still much to do at Ainzara prison to ensure that those committed by the courts were being held in decent conditions and treated in full accordance with human rights. Overall, I did believe, though, that the Prison Service was moving in the right direction and those in charge knew what needed to be done and wanted to do it. It is greatly to the credit of the establishments I visited that there was no attempt to disguise obvious shortcomings. The most significant problem, as expressed by staff and prisoners, was the complete lack of movement through the judicial process, and the struggle with the numbers being held and the prison conditions.

Epilogue

The Prison Service I joined smelled of urine and cabbage, urine because there was lots of it about (in the absence of in-cell sanitation), and the cabbage smell I never understood as cabbage wasn't on the menu more frequently than any other tasteless, overcooked, watery vegetable.

The Prison Service I left smelled of bleach. Sanitation had improved.

The Prison Service I joined treated prisoners as numbers, not people. It was unheard of to address prisoners other than by their number or surname.

The Prison Service I left had developed a sense of decency, which operated both ways with respect, sometimes through gritted teeth, from both sides. As I write, I am only too aware of the huge strains that are impacting on the Prison Service today and threaten the decency agenda that is so crucial in running humane prisons.

The Prison Service I joined had a minor drugs problem and did very little about it. It was not seen as that important.

The Prison Service I left had a significant drugs problem. It is the major barrier to well-functioning rehabilitative prisons and the Prison Service is working very hard to address the problem.

The Prison Service I joined was set in its ways and had been for decades. The approach to prisoners was, 'Give them nothing, and if they complain, take it away from them'.

The Prison Service I left was much more open to change. This more open-minded approach was hard won and down to the efforts of many people over many years.

I am proud to have played a small part in it.